In order that man may satisfy these needs, a new order must be constructed on the application of the Four Freedoms, as reiterated by President Franklin D. Roosevelt, in his message on the State of the Union to the 77th Congress of the United States, January 6, 1941.

FREEDOM THROUGH EDUCATION gives a concise, well-documented answer to the pressing problem on how to concretize the Four Freedoms in everyday American life, now, and in the generations to come.

FREEDOM THROUGH EDUCATION

Freedom
Through Education

By

JOHN D. REDDEN, Ph.D.
School of Education, Fordham University

And

FRANCIS A. RYAN, Ph.D.
School of Education, Fordham University

THE BRUCE PUBLISHING COMPANY
MILWAUKEE

Nihil obstat: ARTHUR J. SCANLON, S.T.D.
Imprimatur: ✠ FRANCIS J. SPELLMAN, D.D., Archbishop of New York
February 24, 1944

WAR FORMAT

Departures from the usual Bruce style in the format of this book
are the result of necessary war conservation of materials and labor.

FOREWORD

MODERN civilization is undergoing what profound thinkers describe as "the gravest crisis in history." The Christian way of life, the democratic ideal, man's inalienable right to "life, liberty, and the pursuit of happiness," are threatened with destruction. The world is at war because certain men and nations, impelled by false philosophies, have refused to accept God's Commandments as directive of all conduct. The forces of atheism and totalitarianism seek to annihilate religion, the Church, and the very foundations of freedom itself. These forces deny the inherent worth of the individual; his God-given rights and duties; his equality before the civil law; and the eternal principles of the moral law which govern individual and social conduct.

These eternal principles, however, must be applied consistently in individual, social, political, economic, and international relationships if a world order founded on universal justice is finally to be established. The forces of religion and democracy are striving at the present time to bring about that world order. They endeavor to defend man's religious freedom, his social and economic freedom, and his freedom of expression. But these freedoms must be interpreted within the law, human and divine. Life outside the law menaces and destroys freedom.

Thus, if the present world turmoil is to end in an

v

enduring peace, the law of God, not the materialistic interpretation of life, must be made to rule the hearts of men. This law alone supplies the principles required for peace with justice throughout the world. These principles proclaim the existence of God; the rule of His divine providence over all things; the immortality of man's soul; the freedom of man's will; his moral responsibility to God, his neighbor, and himself; the intrinsic worth and dignity of the individual; his inalienable rights; and the necessity of respect for and obedience to properly constituted authority.

The central theme of this book is that the truths of right philosophy and divine revelation supply the only valid foundation on which freedom can rest. The recognition of them is essential to the establishment and maintenance of a stable social order. Education will further the ideals of Christian democracy, insure the happiness and well being of the individual, and lay the foundations of international peace with justice.

FRANCIS J. SPELLMAN
Archbishop of New York

February 22, 1944

PREFACE

THE first half of the twentieth century may well be described as the period of confusion and conflict. Individuals, groups, nations have fallen prey to the teachings of false philosophies, and, in consequence, have disagreed concerning man's origin, his nature and destiny; the functions of society and the state; the origin, meaning, and limitations of freedom and authority; the exercise of rights and duties; the norms and sanctions of morality; the meaning and functioning of the democratic way of life; and the nature of the educative process.

The result of this disagreement, arising from false and exclusive views which misinterpret the fundamental truths of life, is confusion in human thought, as has been evidenced by totalitarianism in Germany, fascism in Italy, and unbridled militarism in Japan.

These erroneous philosophies seek the utter destruction of the democratic way of life, the traditional values founded on man's inalienable rights, the moral law, the Four Freedoms, and the teachings of Jesus Christ. The peoples of many sovereign nations have fallen, momentarily, under the yoke of the conqueror, and, enslaved by his materialistic, pragmatic world order, they earnestly await the day of liberation by the United Nations.

To these people, and to each individual everywhere

in the world, the United Nations seek to restore or extend the blessings of the democratic way of life. That way of life is founded and constructed on fundamental truths which offer to a suffering world a new social order based on the Four Freedoms, namely, freedom of speech and expression, freedom of religion, freedom from want, and freedom from fear. This means, in its broadest sense, the reconstruction of a world order in conformity with the pattern implied by the correct meaning and application of these freedoms.

It is the purpose of this book to set forth clearly the proper meaning, scope, and application of the Four Freedoms, and the manner in which they can be implemented appropriately by education. A further purpose is to demonstrate that these freedoms have a moral foundation based on the truths of philosophy and divine revelation; and that they can be put into effective practice only under the democratic way of life, which in the United States is commonly termed "the American way of life." That way of life, if it is to be truly democratic, must be essentially the way taught and exemplified by Jesus Christ. Thus, the democratic way of life, properly interpreted, is the Christian way of life, founded on truths derived from two sources, namely, reason and divine revelation. It is only in the Christian way of life that the Four Freedoms can be properly understood, correctly expressed, and completely enjoyed.

Such is the central theme of this book. The authors have purposely repeated it from time to time whenever, in their opinion, such iteration would serve the reader to fix it firmly in his own mind.

This book should be of interest to the general

reader, to discussion groups, to public officials, educators, and churchmen, since it sets forth the fundamental truths on which alone can be constructed a Christian, democratic, social order. It may be used profitably, also, by teachers for primary or supplementary reading in courses such as Problems of Democracy, Principles of Democracy, Education for Democracy, Social Reconstruction, and Economic Citizenship, because it demonstrates how the Four Freedoms can be implemented by right education, and how they can function effectively in daily living.

JOHN D. REDDEN
FRANCIS A. RYAN

New York, N. Y.
February 2, 1944.

ACKNOWLEDGMENTS

The authors acknowledge their gratitude to His Excellency, The Most Reverend Francis J. Spellman, Archbishop of New York, for writing the Foreword of this book. Thanks are also expressed to Reverend James T. Cronin, Ph.D., School of Education, Fordham University, for his constructive criticism and encouragement. The authors express appreciation to the various authors and publishers for permission to quote materials from certain books and periodicals cited in footnotes.

CONTENTS

Chapter I

THE MEANING OF THE
FOUR FREEDOMS

INTRODUCTION. Future historians may well designate
the first half of the twentieth century as "the period
of confusion." People have been confused about life
and its meaning, about the values of life, and the
guiding principles of conduct. As the poet Tennyson
expressed it: "There is confusion worse than death."
It is the confusion that has sprung from the destruction
of human values by false philosophies of life, and from
the fruitless goals which those philosophies have set up.
With the stones of naturalism, socialism, nationalism,
communism, and experimentalism, men have attempted
to build an arrogant Tower of Babel; and the curse of
the confusion of tongues has fallen, leaving them
bewildered in this valley of the shadow.

This confusion is the inevitable result of false views
of man, the State, society, morality, and education.
Thus, by the experimentalist man is held to be a product of his own experiences, who differs from the animals
in degree but not in kind. For the naturalist, man is
continuous with nature, is produced by the blind evolution of matter, and has neither divine origin nor ultimate end. Communism, based as it is on the fallacious
laws of dialectical materialism, holds that the individual

is merely an evolving form of matter, and interprets the term society to mean the proletariat.

By many today, the State is said to be the supreme institution from which come all of man's rights and to which he owes all his obligations. For these people, the State supplants the family and the Church; the individual exists solely to promote the material welfare and autonomy of the State or nation. Society, they hold, is man-made in its origin; it is the great "reality," the ultimate objective of all human endeavor. Such people regard the individual as merely a product of the group, who exists solely to promote its well-being. All that man is or hopes to be, they say, depends solely on society; and it is the duty of every man to make rapid adjustments to those social practices that serve the "needs" of society, and that contribute to the improvement of the social order.

Morality they interpret as entirely social in origin and devised to serve group interests and purposes. Hence, it is subject to constant change in conformity to social and pragmatic standards.

Education, according to these false thinkers, must serve to indoctrinate the individual in the particular national ideology and pattern, and to facilitate him in the acquisition of those knowledges and skills which will best meet the needs of a changing social order.

From the denial, rejection, or exclusion of a correct interpretation of man, the State, society, morality, and education conflicts, which have spread to world proportions, have arisen among nations. Certain nations seek to uproot and destroy all traditional values based on man's true nature, and on unchanging moral principles evident in the "way of life" taught and exemplified by Christ. They deny, moreover, that man's inalienable rights of life, liberty, and the pursuit of happiness are free gifts from the Creator and basic principles of the natural law. They disregard, fundamentally, the worth of the individual, and, in practice, seek to reduce man to a state of slavery.

Thus, false philosophy in the form of the totalitarian state proclaims that "might is right," "all justice is political," and "the members of this state are a race of supermen destined to rule the world." It is against these false ideals and practices that the United Nations are fighting. These latter have marshaled their total resources in a supreme effort to preserve and propagate the democratic way of life by the destruction of totalitarianism with all its pernicious ideology and baneful ramifications. Upon the completion of this destruction, the democratic way of life, which in reality is the Christian concept of society, can be restored or extended to all people everywhere in the world through the Four Freedoms, properly interpreted and implemented by right education.

The true meaning and import of these freedoms are denied by false philosophies. Each in its own characteristic manner proposes a program of social reconstruction for postwar years based on its own exclusive interpretation. Such proposals, in the main, are in conflict with true philosophy because they present false views of man, society, and morality.

It follows that any program of social reconstruction, if true amelioration is to be achieved, must envisage the basic needs of man, embrace a correct notion of society, accord with predetermined standards of morality, conform in every detail to God's law and plan, and

contribute to man's material and spiritual development. This development requires that man be assisted,
in every reasonable way, to attain the following needs:
(1) eternal life for his soul; (2) truth about himself,
his world, and his eternal destiny; (3) goodness,
whereby the will freely chooses to conform in conduct
to eternal verities through love of God and love of
neighbor; (4) material well-being sufficient to enable
him to realize and to promote his legitimate vocational
ambitions.

In order that man may satisfy these needs, a new
order must be constructed on the application of the
Four Freedoms. President Franklin D. Roosevelt, in his
message on the State of the Union to the 77th Congress
of the United States, January 6, 1941, voiced his hope
for a world in the future founded on a "moral order."
This order "under the guidance of God," wherein
freedom implies "the supremacy of human rights
everywhere," is opposed to the so-called new order of
tyranny proposed by the totalitarian states. The
precious objective to be gained in the peace that is
to be won following the conclusion of World War II
is "a new world order" fashioned from the groundwork
of four essential freedoms. In the words of President
Roosevelt:

In the future days, which we seek to make secure, we
look forward to a world founded upon four essential human
freedoms.

The first is freedom of speech and expression everywhere in the world.

The second is freedom of every person to worship God
in his own way everywhere in the world.

The third is freedom from want, which, translated into
world terms, means economic understandings which will

secure to every nation a healthy peacetime life for its inhabitants everywhere in the world.

The fourth is freedom from fear — which, translated into world terms, means a world-wide reduction of armaments to such a point and in such a thorough fashion that no nation will be in a position to commit an act of physical aggression against any neighbor — anywhere in the world.[1]

It is important at the outset that the exact meaning of freedom itself, as well as the meaning of each of the Four Freedoms, be made clear. Each must further be limited as to scope and application, so that proposals for its implementation by education may be intelligently understood and adequately planned. Such definition and limitation, therefore, must be stated in terms of right philosophy, which supplies the only valid interpretation of these freedoms.

THE MEANING OF FREEDOM. Freedom implies the capacity to choose morally. To make this choice the individual must be able to discern between what is right and what is wrong. It is a well-known but often disputed fact that the will of man is free. By virtue of this divine endowment, the will is physically free to choose among and between motives, to select good or evil. But while the will is physically free, it is not morally free, because man is responsible for his conduct. If he chooses evil, his conduct is sinful and deserves condemnation. If he chooses good, his conduct is virtuous and merits reward. Freedom means, then, the ability to do what one ought to do; that is, to do what is right, just, lawful, and to avoid what is evil. In other words, *freedom means man's power within himself to act in conformity to his rational nature.*

---

[1] Roosevelt, President Franklin D., "Message to 77th Congress of the United States on the State of the Union," *Congressional Record,* Vol. 87, Jan. 6, 1941, p. 54.

Hoffman draws a distinction between freedom and liberty in the following passage:

Between the words *liberty* and *freedom* . . . there is an important difference. Liberty denotes that set of conditions or circumstances wherein a person may act from choice, as it pleases that person — the sphere of unconstrained action, in which one meets with no external compulsions or prohibitions. Freedom, on the other hand, is a subjective conception. It designates a consciousness in us of what we are, an inner illumination of our nature whereby we know ourselves as moral agents, able to discern right and wrong and to exercise the power of moral choice. In this sense no man is free who does not know himself as being possessed of free will. Our Lord, it will be remembered, did not say the truth would set us at liberty, but that it would make us free. For liberty may be conferred from without, as a slave is emancipated or a prisoner discharged, but freedom can be had only by men who know what kind of creatures God fashioned them to be.[2]

Properly speaking, then, freedom does not mean that a man may do as he pleases. Rather, it means his ability and obligation to do what sound reason and morality teach him he *ought* to do in order best to fulfill the social, civic, and spiritual purposes for which he was created. The term "ought" is the norm in the correct interpretation of freedom, which, makes the fact perfectly clear that freedom has a *moral* foundation. Hence, it should be emphasized that freedom is a moral potency directed in application and scope by moral and religious principles, and that it is not a mere physical potency founded on the social will, and subject to the passing whims of a changing social order.

---

[2] Hoffman, R., *Tradition and Progress* (Milwaukee: The Bruce Publishing Co., 1938), p. 103.

Freedom is founded on eternal truths; on man's inner powers and inalienable rights. These do not change with the passing of time, nor are they subject to the accidental conditions of time, place, or circumstance. Man's powers and rights are gifts from his Creator; and the freedom to use and enjoy these gifts must always be exercised by the individual in conformity to the natural law, which exists outside of man, and with solicitude for the rights of his fellow men. Thus, the greatest degree of freedom for the individual may often be had when, in the interests of his neighbors to whom he is bound by the common bond of humanity, he sacrifices certain rights to which he is legitimately entitled.

Both experience and reason show that there can be no true freedom when the moral principles on which freedom rests are denied or excluded. In truth and fact it is these very principles that make freedom possible. Without them, man would be enslaved by his own desires, emotions, and selfish, conflicting interests. To do as one pleases, which is extreme liberalism, induces unbridled license together with individual and social conflict. This false notion of freedom gives free rein to man's inherent weaknesses which, by his very nature, incline him to evil.

Another false notion of freedom is held by the modern advocates of determinism. According to determinism, man's conduct results from the combination of past experiences, forces, and external conditions over which he has no control, or which predetermine his behavior patterns. Thus, the determinists hold that heredity, environment, social processes, economic factors, scientific techniques, and many other complex stimuli converge on man and can be made to explain his every act. The determinists, furthermore, deny freedom of choice because they assert that, in consequence of previous behavior patterns with their resultant strengthened neural pathways ready to produce a satisfying state of affairs, man is not free to select his course of action. Rather, he *must* respond to the combined stimuli of his past and present, which condition him according to a definite pattern. Since the present is said to be the outcome of the past, so also the present, according to the determinists, effectively conditions the future. Given an accurate chart of the stimuli brought to bear on the individual, the determinist asserts that he can predict unfailingly the course of the individual's future behavior. Thus, the freedom of the will is denied. No recognition is given to the fact that, frequently, an individual, by virtue of his power of volition, can hold out against the strongest combinations of stimuli, and thus prove that he is not merely the sum of all his experiences and habits. Determinism would reduce man to the status of a mechanism dominated by stimulus-response bonds, and fatally destined to live and die "on the scaffolding of unyielding despair."

To do what one *ought,* not because of the power to do as one pleases, or what one must, or what one's experiences and inclinations crave, but rather because such conduct comports with one's rational nature and is right and just, is the only concept of freedom which is reasonably tenable. Freedom always depends on obedience to law, and can exist only within the law.

Leo XIII explains the correct relation between law and freedom as follows:

Such then being the condition of human liberty, it necessarily stands in need of light and strength to direct its actions to good and to restrain them from evil. Without this the freedom of our will would be our ruin. First of all there must be *law;* that is, a fixed rule of teaching concerning what is to be done and what is to be left undone. . . . In other words, the reason prescribes to the will what it should seek after or shun, in order to pursue the eventual attainment of man's last end, for the sake of which all his actions ought to be performed. This ordination of *reason* is called law. In man's free will, therefore, or in the moral necessity that our voluntary acts must be in accordance with reason, lies the very root of the necessity of law. Nothing more foolish can be uttered or conceived than the notion that because man is free by nature, he is therefore exempt from law. Were this the case, it would follow that to become free we must be deprived of reason; whereas the truth is that we are bound to submit to law precisely because we are free by our very nature.[3]

FREEDOM AND AUTHORITY. The modern struggle for freedom is sometimes directed, mistakenly, against the imposition on the human intellect of any authoritative mode of thought. Among many people today there is a flight from authority. Yet, it is an inescapable fact that a definite and necessary relationship exists between rightly constituted authority and the knowledge of what is true freedom. As stated earlier in this chapter, freedom means the ability to do what one *ought* to do in conformity to his rational nature. Now, in order to know what one *ought* to do, it is necessary, first of all, to know what is true; what is right and what is wrong; what is good and what is evil. The proper object of the human intellect is, as the philosophers say, *truth.*

[3] Leo XIII, *Libertas Humana, Social Wellsprings* (Milwaukee: The Bruce Publishing Co., 1940), pp. 118, 119.

There is no question of authority when the intellect has its assent forced upon itself, as it were, by the very fact of a self-evident truth. A great number of truths, however, are not self-evident. Those truths are capable of evidence, but that evidence is not immediately grasped by the intellect. Such evidence will remain beyond the reach of the individual's intellect until some person in authority, or some authoritative agency, sets out systematically to present that evidence. For example, the beginner in the study of the sciences cannot perceive immediately, without the aid of a mature, competent adult, the evidence of scientific demonstrations. He must rely, at first, on the guidance and authority of his teacher. Indeed, a long period of time may have to elapse before this beginner recognizes immediately, and without aid, the truth of the evidence. Until his intellect is able to give a firm assent to the evidence of the truths which he perceives on the authority of his teacher, the beginner will make little progress in his scientific studies. Hence, the authority of the teacher must *substitute,* momentarily, for the evidence of the demonstration itself.

Since adults are, in the main, merely "children of a larger growth," this same condition of beginner often applies to them. There are truths in the moral order, as well as in the scientific world, which must be accepted on authority. Some scientific and moral truths are known only by the most learned; they remain forever unknown or inexplicable to the average person. Likewise, in the spiritual order, there are truths which, directly concerned with man's salvation, are entrusted to the authority of the Catholic Church. No one in this material world can have a full perception of them;

that full perception will be revealed later in the beatific vision. In this case, faith based on authority must *substitute,* as it were, for exact and full knowledge. Authority, then, at times, must necessarily substitute temporarily for freedom in those matters wherein proper temporal and spiritual good make reasonably evident the necessity for substitution

Authority is a necessary limitation to freedom, also, when the individual is unable or unwilling to govern himself. The lives of most people would be continually imperiled, and would end in complete disaster, were it not for the authority which daily encompasses them and guarantees the exercise of their freedom.

Authority, then, has certain definite functions in regard to freedom. These functions are three in number: (1) the substitutional function; (2) the essential function; and (3) the perfective function.

1. THE SUBSTITUTIONAL FUNCTION. This function is made necessary because of some deficiency either in man's nature, or in the progress of his development from immaturity to maturity, or, again, in some element of his environment. Such authority usually tends to disappear according as the individual's rational nature enables him to direct his own conduct intelligently. This does not apply, of course, to truths in the spiritual order.

2. THE ESSENTIAL FUNCTION. This function is directed to the common good, and often the highest good, of the social group. Even under ideal conditions this function is necessary because, in any social group, the concerted action of the group must be directed to that good. In other words, each individual of the group must work for the benefit of all; submit himself and his

action to the common good; but, without authority, either persuasive or coercive, some individuals would fail to do this. Hence, authority is necessary or essential in the group to attain the common good. This is what is meant, then, by the *essential function* of authority. Such authority is *essential* to the welfare of the group, and is derived from the very nature of society itself.

3. THE PERFECTIVE FUNCTION. Even in a social group capable of the highest degree of self-government and self-direction, wherein all minds and efforts are directed unquestionably to the common good, the function of authority is still necessary. This is evident from the fact that, in such a group, there are always those who are less endowed with intelligence, who lack experience, and whose wills are not controlled by self-discipline. These people must be guided by those who are more fortunately endowed, who are richer in experience, and who have learned through many trials to discipline themselves. Here, authority is not essentially necessary, but it is *perfective* of the highest common good. This is what is meant by the perfective function of authority.

Each of these functions, far from being a limitation to freedom, should be regarded, fundamentally, as aids to the proper exercise of freedom, since they serve to enable the individual to do those things which, in conformity to his rational nature, he *ought* to do. This power to do what one ought to do as a rational human being is freedom in its true meaning. It is only on this true meaning of freedom that the Four Freedoms themselves, which will now be discussed, can be intelligently achieved.

1. FREEDOM OF SPEECH AND EXPRESSION. The first

of the four freedoms proclaimed by President Roosevelt, namely, freedom of speech, is a natural right possessed only by man. This natural right implies the recognition of the moral and legal liberty, subject to definite limitations, for an individual to express his ideas, opinions, hopes, vocational choices and pursuits without undue interference from his fellow men, society, or the State.

Speech is an attribute of the human being, because man is the only animal capable of making articulate sounds to express his ideas, developing these sounds into language, and communicating his ideas thereby to others. This capacity is but one evidence of the existence of man's rational soul, and demonstrates one manner in which his intellect operates. In order that man's intellect may attain its proper object, namely, truth, which serves to enlighten his will in the choice of good, ideas and judgments must be formed before they can be communicated. But language is the medium of communication of those ideas and judgments. It is one of the most important means of social intercourse by which man can transmit his ideas and profit likewise by the ideas of others. It is an essential in all social life, group cooperation, and representative government. Hence, language and its correct use are a necessary tool for the fulfillment of man's purposes, material and spiritual.

There are numerous things in human affairs, of a purely material aspect, capable of various individual interpretations. By the use of free speech in such instances, enlightened opinions and creative ideas developed out of individual experiences may be gained. Expression of opinions, moreover, frequently results in better understanding of contemporary problems, and discussion of these problems from various points of view often promotes their actual solution. Through such discussion, the expression of personal opinions and suggestions at times proves of inestimable value, and frequently brings to light the truth. The use of free speech in this way ordinarily violates no moral or civil law, nor is the common good endangered. On the contrary, the common good is thereby often advanced.

Leo XIII states the function of opinion in the following words:

In regard, however, to any matters of opinion which God leaves to man's free discussion, full liberty of thought and of speech is naturally within the right of everyone; *for such liberty never leads men to suppress the truth,* but often to discover it and make it known.[4]

Since freedom of speech is a natural right, its exercise or enjoyment must be restricted or limited only according to the degree to which the common good is promoted by such limitation. By the common good is meant the fostering and protecting of the material and spiritual welfare of all in such manner that each can pursue with security and safety his material and spiritual purposes. Speech in itself is a tool, a means of exchange of ideas, by which man communicates with others, and, through the medium of prayer, with God, thus contributing to his material and spiritual well-being.

As a right to be enjoyed, speech implies a duty. This duty imposes the obligation to use speech according to its true purpose. Thus, the principle of

---

[4] Leo XIII, *op. cit.,* p. 130 (italics ours).

determining whether or not speech is to be free in a given circumstance must be interpreted according to the exact use to which speech is applied. In the social order, this means that the norm is the degree to which the common welfare is promoted and fostered, provided that no moral-religious principles are violated. Whenever speech would injure this welfare, or be used in a manner that would be morally wrong, the exercise of the right of free speech should and must be restricted. It follows, then, that language, written and spoken, must subserve the attainment of truth and justice, for the promotion of which societies, states, and governments were instituted.

The right of freedom of speech, therefore, does not mean that anyone may say whatever he pleases and when he pleases. The gift of speech was not given to the individual so that he might give vent to every idle fancy of his imagination, or to some perverted urge toward the overthrow of civil law, government, religion, or moral principles. The gift of freedom of speech was not given to utter slander, to calumniate, or to injure the reputation of another person. Speech was not given to be used to thwart or defeat the pursuit of truth and justice, which alone guarantee infallibly man's individual, social, and spiritual perfection. Freedom of speech, therefore, can never be interpreted properly to mean unbridled license whereby the use of this power may undermine truth, flout goodness, outrage public decency and morality, propagate and diffuse racial hatreds and prejudices, disseminate seditious ideas and practices, or jeopardize the material and spiritual well-being of any individual, group, race or nation.

There are certain "highly educated" but misguided

individuals today, as in former days, who crassly misinterpret the meaning and end of freedom in general
and freedom of speech in particular. These individuals
plead that right and wrong should receive equal
emphasis in oral and written expression; that eventually, because of its pragmatic and instrumental value,
the truth will triumph. The individual, they say, can
discern for himself what is true and right and good;
hence, no restriction should be placed on freedom
of speech. They hold, moreover, that the individual
creates his own truth, and is not influenced to any
appreciable degree by oratory, cogent emotional appeals,
the moral law, or social controls. The foregoing false
notion of freedom of speech ignores the inherent effects
of man's fallen but redeemed nature with its consequent
limitations, which make him less able to attain truth,
less able to seek good, and more inclined to evil. It
fails to consider the need for the influence of maturity
over immaturity, and of wisdom over folly, in order that
the individual may receive that necessary guidance
which will insure right development of all his powers
and their correct discipline. It fails, moreover, to recognize the dignity of man and the worth of personality.
Furthermore, truth is not put forward and error excluded. When truth and right receive equal position
with error and wrong, the concepts governing duty,
moral responsibility, and personal integrity tend to be
weakened, gradually thwarted, and progress in the social
order is impeded.

By virtue of his inherent limitations, man may be
deceived and accept as true something which is wholly
wrong, because that particular thing appears to have
some good. It may be injurious to his material and

spiritual welfare, but is accepted because of the dictum of someone who has spoken with the oratorical effectiveness of an expert. Thus, the point of view of such a speaker may be accepted as authoritative by the uninitiated without any question or hesitation. An illustration of this fact is found in the number of well-meaning Americans who have fallen prey to the promises and vaunted hopes set forth by communism. These Americans hope to acquire certain apparent goods or values, such as greater opportunities to enjoy rights, higher wages, shorter hours of employment, etc. These same Americans are deceived by this abuse of the right of free speech. Stimulated by false promises of greater wealth, more worldly goods, and physical comfort, these people clamor for more individual liberties and the removal of personal restrictions. They forget that the enjoyment of rights always requires the acceptance of duties and responsibilities. They forget, furthermore, that it is not only the expression of certain ideas that proves harmful, but also the tendency for these ideas to be diffused and accepted because of ignorance, shortsightedness, or ill will.

Freedom of expression always implies the free choice and pursuit of one's vocation or avocation, consonant with the moral law, without fear of regimentation by governmental authority. One of its proper functions is to prevent, among other things, forced labor and the economic, social, and moral ills that flow from the degradation of the workingman by physical or mental coercion. Likewise, it seeks to prevent the evils that have their source in nationalistic, racial, financial, and capitalistic selfishness or greed. An added function, moreover, concerns the free expression of the individual's legitimate purposes, creative talents, and social interests, to the end that he may contribute to his own material and spiritual welfare, and to the promotion of the common good.

The same fundamental principles that govern speech and expression govern the freedom of the press. There is a limit to every freedom man possesses. When a freedom is abused, that abuse constitutes license. It is possible, and sometimes quite probable, that the press itself may, consciously or unconsciously, abuse its freedom. This abuse is caused by the insatiable thirst for "news," which the press frequently displays. Now, the chief function of the press is the dispassionate, impartial statement and dissemination of truth. But truth is not infrequently sacrificed because a particular newspaper, or a syndicate, prefers to tickle the public curiosity and fancy, or whet the public appetite for sensational appeal. The public gets its information, and forms most of its opinions and convictions, from the daily press and periodicals. Hence, these latter have a most grave responsibility and obligation. When the press recognizes the basic principles of freedom of speech and expression, and observes the reasonable limitations which govern that freedom, then the press becomes a tower of strength for truth, justice, and freedom.

At times, freedom of the press is extremely difficult to define. It is often impossible to put one's finger on specific instances and say: "This instance is freedom; that instance is license or abuse." On the other hand, one may very safely and properly say that the press is not permitted, under the concept of freedom, to publish a deliberate lie. Indeed, laws exist to give redress to the injured in such an instance. Again, were

the press to argue for or defend a change in duly constituted government by other than peaceful means, it
would be exceeding the limits of its freedom. Furthermore, if the press were to attack a racial or religious
group, simply on the basis of race or religion, it would
be guilty of a grave abuse. Likewise, if the press were to
attack properly constituted government and attempt to
substitute in its place, a collectivistic, socialistic, or communistic order, it would again be guilty of abuse of its
freedom. Also the press has no right whatsoever to "try
a case" in its columns before that case is tried by the
court, or during the procedure of the trial. Finally, the
press ought not to publish material that is offensive to
morality and religion, and that outrages public decency.

When the press puts forth facts, truth, and exercises
tolerance and self-restraint, it is living up to the ideal
of its freedom. When, however, it disregards facts, cares
nothing about truth, and uses its instrumentality for
selfish, sensational, vindictive ends, or merely for ends
that are financially profitable to it at the expense of
truth and justice, then the press abuses the freedom
which makes its very existence possible.

2. FREEDOM OF EVERY PERSON TO WORSHIP GOD
IN HIS OWN WAY. In order to acquire the correct
meaning and full import of this God-given right, one
must understand man, his purpose, and last end. As
true philosophy shows, man was divinely created. He
exists to praise, reverence, and serve God. By living the
good life, fighting the good fight, he can earn eternal
happiness with his Creator. To attain this ultimate
end man must love God, love his neighbor, abide by
and uphold truth, justice, and charity in all his
individual and social relations.

Man is endowed by his Creator with certain powers and inalienable rights. By the exercise of these according to their proper ends, he may fulfill the purpose of his creation. Man must *earn* his eternal reward by right individual and social conduct. The fundamental norm in all conduct is the eternal law of God made known to man by conscience. Conscience is the judgment one makes of the rightness or wrongness of a human act, i.e., an act that one is free to do or not to do. Conscience accuses or excuses human acts, and points out man's obligation to do good and avoid evil. It must be refined and strengthened so that it will face truth and reality without fear, restraint, or distortion, and will always point to the norms governing the individual's ultimate good. Divine revelation, furthermore, has clearly made known to man how to conform his life completely to the norms set up by the eternal law. Conscience informs the individual how closely his life conforms to those norms.

In addition to conscience, man needs a strongly disciplined will to overcome the temptations to evil arising from "the world, the flesh, and the devil." This may be achieved in part by the enlightenment of the will through right ideas supplied by the intellect and by explicit instruction, training, and practice in conformity to these ideas. Thus, man can attain through his own efforts, aided by grace, something of that "rectitude" which was his before the fall.

Because of original sin, man suffered certain deprivations and found himself in what is called "a fallen state." Through the merits of Jesus Christ, "by whose stripes we are healed," man was redeemed from this fallen state. Certain preternatural privileges, however, were not restored to him; namely, bodily immortality and perfect control of his natural desires. Consequently, man possesses an intellect less able to attain truth than in the preternatural state and in need of enlightenment; a will less able to seek the good and in need of being strengthened by discipline; and a human nature more inclined to evil and in need of self-control. Despite these limitations, man by discipline and right living can lessen these consequences, and approach as nearly as it is humanly possible to his eternal perfection here on earth. But to this end, he must have infallible knowledge about the present and the future world, his role and purpose therein, and the right way of life to attain his ultimate happiness. In this double striving for truth and happiness, religion serves as the infallible guide. It offers not only the eternal truths governing life and man's ultimate end, but it also presents a perfect model in the life and teachings of Christ.

It is only by behavior which conforms to religious truths and to the way of life taught therein, that material and spiritual perfection can be attained. Man seeks the highest form of truth for his intellect and the highest form of good for his will; he can find the complete object of his search only in the knowledge and practice of religion. Natural science and human reason, in themselves, have failed to explain completely man's purposes here on earth and the means to attain his ultimate end. Divinely revealed religion alone supplies the complete answer to the final what, how, why, Who. Because of the infallibility of divinely revealed truths man can go forward in life with certainty and freedom. Since man must gain his eternal end, and since religion alone can enable him to do so, therefore, he must have freedom of religion.

Freedom to worship God is the inalienable right, therefore, of every person everywhere in the world. With this right, however, goes a corresponding duty. Since God is the Creator and man is His creature, it is the duty of the creature to acknowledge his Creator, and to worship Him "in spirit and in truth." This worship of God must follow the dictates of one's conscience, rightly disciplined, refined, and subject always to ultimate truth, justice, and goodness. No person, nation, State, or society can rightfully deny any man the exercise of this duty. In the final analysis, man is responsible to God for his conduct, and the salvation of his immortal soul depends upon the manner in which he lives according to God's law and exercises his right to worship his Creator.

Man has a further obligation imposed on him by this particular freedom. Not only must he worship God, but he must also direct his intellect and his heart to the discovery of the *right* way to worship God: the way that God Himself has revealed through the life and teachings of His divine Son, Jesus Christ. It is not sufficient, therefore, that man worship God merely in a free and easy way, according to his personal tastes and his own individual interpretation. Since freedom, rightly interpreted, means the liberty and power to do what one *ought* to do as a rational being, it is evident that a vital obligation which this freedom of worship imposes on man is that of seeking the truth, as far as it is humanly possible for him. This obligation weighs all the more heavily on man according as truth is more intimately connected with his last end and highest good. Thus, man is obliged to try to discover, among the various religions in the world, the one *true* religion which God Himself has revealed to man by certain marks or characteristics that cause it to be easily recognized. Leo XIII describes the right and duty to worship God as follows:

> But, assuredly, of all the duties which man has to fulfil, that, without doubt, is the chiefest and holiest which commands him to worship God with devotion and piety. This follows of necessity from the truth that we are ever in the power of God, are ever guided by His will and providence, and, having come forth from Him, must return to Him. Add to which no true virtue can exist without religion. For moral virtue is concerned with those things which lead to God as man's supreme and ultimate good. Therefore religion, which (as St. Thomas says) "performs those actions which are directly and immediately ordained for the divine honor" (*Summa*, 2ᵃ 2ᵃᵉ, q. lxxxi, a. 6), rules and tempers all virtues. And if it be asked which of the many conflicting religions it is necessary to adopt, reason and the natural law unhesitatingly tell us to practice that one which God enjoins, and which men can easily recognize by certain exterior notes, whereby divine Providence has willed that it should be distinguished, because, in a matter of such moment, the most terrible loss would be the consequence of error. Wherefore, when a liberty such as we have described is offered to man, the power is given him to pervert or abandon with impunity the most sacred of duties, and to exchange the unchangeable good for evil; which, as we have said, is not liberty, but its degradation, and the abject submission of the soul to sin.[5]

Freedom to worship God implies, in its correct meaning and application, that every man should acknowledge

---

[5] Leo XIII, *op. cit.*, pp. 127–128.

God as his Creator, submit to His divine rule and will, and, through the proper use of faith and reason, embrace those eternal truths which alone insure salvation. This is true freedom. It is opposed to that so-called "liberty of conscience" which a "seditious and rebellious mind," dominated by man's lower nature and blinded to truth and goodness, employs to undermine, overthrow, or destroy the infallible authority of religion to govern and direct all the individual's conduct in terms of the moral law. This latter notion of freedom would deny the moral law and the need for discipline and authority, because it holds that the individual is free to worship God or not to worship Him, or even to attempt to prevent others from worshiping Him. Because of the frequently intolerant attitude toward the Church and the teachings of religion, this "liberty of conscience" tends to pervert the true notion of freedom. To deny God's authority, or refuse to abide by the injunctions of His law, is not to act as a free man; rather, it is to be enslaved by the forces of evil and corruption. If an individual is to be truly free, the words of Christ must ever guide him: "If you continue in my word, you shall be my disciples indeed. And you shall know the truth, and the truth shall make you free" (John 8:31, 32).

3. FREEDOM FROM WANT. Because freedom implies ability to choose what is right and just, in the use of freedom man must conform always to the true purposes of his rational nature. He was put on earth for a definite reason: proximately to live in peace, harmony, and justice with his fellow men under the law of God, and ultimately to attain supreme goodness through

union with his Creator. Sound reasoning shows that everything, worldly goods, all liberties and rights, must subserve this ultimate end. Now freedom from want is one of those liberties whereby man has a right to gain a sufficiency of various material and spiritual goods so that no aspect of his nature will be neglected, and so that, by proper use of these goods, his ultimate purpose will be fulfilled. This means that the individual should be given every opportunity, consonant with the right use of this freedom, to seek and possess those goods to which his nature legitimately inclines, and which are requisite to his economic satisfaction as well as his attainment of the goal of life, namely, the universal good.

Because the meaning and scope of this third freedom must be governed by and conformed to the right concept of "goodness," it is essential that the correct notion of what "goodness" means should clearly be made known. Redden and Ryan describe goodness as follows:

Goodness may be defined in general as that property or quality of being toward which all things tend, namely, that which is desirable or which has an *appetitive* appeal. *Bonum est quod omnia appetunt.* A being tends toward some good, because that object or pattern is suitable or attractive in that it possesses something capable of *perfecting* the being desiring it.

Goodness, therefore, implies a relation of suitability to some nature. It must, indeed, be something positive, for only a positive thing can be the object of a desire. But one cannot conclude that every being is good in every respect, for such would constitute a denial of the fact of evil. One must distinguish between a *good* (something desirable, without regard to its moral quality) and *a moral good* (something desirable and at the same time morally good in itself).

Good has various subdivisions such as physical and moral, absolute and relative, etc.[6]

Of all created things, man alone can consciously set up his purposes, goals, and the objects of labor, strive to achieve them, freely choose the means to reach them, and thus attain for himself the various goods included therein. For his soul, man seeks the universal good, namely, spiritual sanctification, union with his Creator. For his intellect he seeks the highest truth; and for his will the ultimate good. For his body, man seeks the satisfaction of the proper objects of his senses by securing those goods which bring his physical nature to the highest state of perfection.

The satisfaction of physical, intellectual, and volitional needs or wants of man, which must tend to perfect his "whole being" by the pursuit of appropriate "good," must always be subordinated to the spiritual and must subserve its "needs." In his response to primary biological wants, such as food, shelter, clothing, self-preservation, self-propagation — all good in themselves when pursued according to their proper object — man must at all times be guided by principles of truth and justice. These biological wants are means to his spiritual sanctification, and must not be permitted to become ends dominated by selfishness, license, and uncontrolled appetite. It should be remembered that a thing is good for man only if it be in accord with his rational nature and final purpose. If the thing be physical, delectable, apparent, or relative good, its pursuit and acceptance must be judged always in the light of its contribution to the perfection of man's rational nature

---

[6] Redden, J. D., and Ryan, F. A., *A Catholic Philosophy of Education* (Milwaukee: The Bruce Publishing Co., 1942), p. 298.

and the common welfare of society. Man's strongest desire is for happiness in the full and complete meaning of
the term. The attainment of this happiness, namely,
eternal life, is in reality the perfection of his nature,
the reason for his existence. Hence, when one speaks
of freedom from want one does not imply that mere
betterment of his worldly affairs, absence of poverty
and hunger, can liberate man from the wants that his
soul will always crave. Such liberation is not found
in this world; it takes place only when man joins his
Creator in the life of eternal bliss. Again, freedom
from want does not mean wants of the body or of
society alone, for these may sometimes imperil the
attainment of man's more essential spiritual wants,
unless the pursuit of those material wants is subjected
to right reason and the injunctions of the moral law.

To acquire wealth, to attend a theatrical performance,
may be in themselves neither good nor evil. Goodness
and badness are determined by the motives, uses,
circumstances, and ends employed by human beings.
The possession of wealth may provide means to obtain
goods which are desirable in themselves and serve to
improve one's standard of living and that of others.
St. Thomas Aquinas holds that a certain amount of
economic comfort is necessary for the practice of virtue.

Ad bonam autem unius hominis vitam duo requiruntur:
unum principale, quod est operatio secundum virtutem
(virtus enim est qua bene vivitur); aliud vero secundarium
et quasi instrumentale, scilicet corporalium bonorum suffi-
cientia, quorum usus est necessarius ad actum virtutis.[7]

---

[7] Aquinas, St. Thomas, *De Regimine Principum* (Taurini, Italy:
Petri Marietti, 1924), Lib. I, Caput XV, p. 22.

The following paraphrase of this passage from St. Thomas is given by Monsignor Fulton J. Sheen.

Two things are necessary for the well-being of man: the first and principal thing consists in acting virtuously; the second is to have a sufficiency of material goods, which is necessary for the exercise of virtue.[8]

On the other hand, abuses of wealth, such as, for example, the oppression of the poor, the satisfaction of self while others are hungry, the denial to labor of a just and living wage, the selfish economic control of food supplies in anticipation of higher profits, all these are essentially wrong and constitute violations of the moral law. Attendance at a theatrical performance may produce a delectable good such as recreation, relaxation, or cultural edification. If such attendance, however, contributes to the support of presentations which corrupt morals and outrage public decency, it must be condemned because it is *morally* wrong. There is, then, a right and a wrong way by which man may seek the satisfaction of his wants, and by which he may employ the goods or means that he has earned, or inherited.

From the foregoing analysis of the correct meaning of the third freedom, it is clear that there is a *right* way in which this freedom may be expressed. That right way should be encouraged and protected. There is also a *wrong* way in which this freedom may be used. That wrong way must be prevented and denied.

Addressing the Congress, January 7, 1943, President Roosevelt stated his own interpretation of freedom from want in the following words:

The people at home, and the people at the front — men

---

[8] Sheen, F. J., *Freedom Under God* (Milwaukee: The Bruce Publishing Co., 1940), p. 107.

and women — are wondering about the third freedom — freedom from want. To them it means that when they are mustered out, when war production is converted to the economy of peace, they will have the right to expect full employment — for themselves and for all able-bodied men and women in America who want to work.

They expect the opportunity to work, to run their farms, their stores, to earn decent wages. They are eager to face the risks inherent in our system of free enterprise.

They do not want a postwar America which suffers from undernourishment or slums — or the dole. They want no get-rich-quick era of bogus "prosperity," which will end for them in selling apples on a street corner, as happened after the bursting of the boom in 1929.

When you talk with our young men and women you will find they want to work for themselves and their families; they consider they have the right to work; and they know that after the last war their fathers did not gain that right.

When you talk with our young men and women you will find that with the opportunity for employment they want assurance against the evils of all major economic hazards — assurance that will extend from the cradle to the grave. This great government can and must provide this assurance.[9]

That steps have been taken by the United States government to implement freedom from want is evident from an examination of the various social security laws already passed, and those measures still pending before Congress. These laws provide among other things: unemployment compensation, old-age security, child welfare services, extension of public health services.[10] The report of Sir William Beveridge in England, which, most likely, will affect future social security legislation in the United States, presents a plan for the implemen-

---

[9] *Congressional Record,* Vol. 89, No. 2, January 7, 1943, p. 47.
[10] Cf. *Social Security in America,* also *Compilation of the Social Security Laws, 1940* (Washington D. C.: Social Security Board).

tation of freedom from want by seeking to effect the solution of social problems "from the cradle to the grave."[11]

Under the accidental conditions of time and place, variations in the interpretation and use of "freedom from want" are justified. These variations do not affect the moral or spiritual principles basic to this freedom, because such principles never change, and are always binding on all men. The opportunity to labor at one's calling, the exact amount of a living wage, as well as the norms governing a decent standard of living, may vary from place to place according to customs, national ideals, culture, geographical location, and the natural resources of a particular nation, state, or community. Again, within a geographical area or social unit, differences may appear between the standard of living maintained in the cities and that of the rural districts, so that what might be actual want in the one situation might be abundance or luxury in the other. In every instance, however, a purposeful attempt must be made to apply the basic principles governing the correct interpretation of freedom in general and freedom from want in particular. In other words, whenever this freedom from want is exercised, care must be taken to produce specifically and actually the maximum common good consonant with the highest good governing truth and justice. The foregoing limitations must be applied in the exercise of this third freedom especially in the postwar period.

4. FREEDOM FROM FEAR. This fourth freedom, which in modern times has been frequently violated by

---

[11] Beveridge, W., *Social Insurance and Allied Services* (New York: The Macmillan Co., 1943).

unjust aggression and the hostile ambitions of the forces of "might" and irreligion, has its salutary aspects and its harmful aspects. Each aspect must be understood correctly and through education fostered or dispelled, so that "freedom from fear" may be accorded proper meaning, place, and importance, as one of the instruments to maintain world peace and individual security. At the same time, it should be made clear that, strictly speaking, man can never be *entirely* free from fear, because fear is inherent in his original nature. To fail to recognize the right meaning and purpose of fear, and to attempt to eliminate it, would result in a collapse of the sanctions basic to morality, authority, law, reason, and justice. Should such collapse occur, fear itself would increase immeasurably, because these sanctions, properly acknowledged and revered, produce the most complete assurance and practical application of freedom from fear.

Fear, then, is an integral part of man's nature. This original tendency was implanted in man by the Creator for a definite purpose, namely, to serve as a means of self-preservation and as a sanction to discipline man and make him conform in conduct to the injunctions of law and authority. Thus, "the fear of the Lord is the beginning of wisdom," a truth which is attested by numerous statements and instances found in the Old and the New Testament. The philosopher Plato taught that fear and anger are the supreme dynamos of action. According to him, anger is "the supreme affirmation of the will to live," and fear, "the supreme negation" of any attempt to threaten or imperil that will to live.

Fear, therefore, serves as a powerful means to regulate man's behavior so that civil, moral, and eternal laws are observed, thereby preserving man's integrity of body and soul. Fear is the mental anguish caused by anticipated physical or intellectual pain, the pain of deprivation, or the loss of God's grace and blessing. This pain may follow in the immediate present or be reserved to the remote future; it may be real or imaginary; it may or may not be attributable to factors within a person's control. Fear implies, usually, a physical and mental state of insecurity in which there is threatened pain or evil consequences from some superior force or power, real or simulated. It is provoked and accentuated by an intellectual state of doubt concerning the truth or consequences, the rightness, wrongness, or *oughtness* of one's actions, and there is absent a definite standard of judgment which excludes the possibility of error. Thus, under fear certitude is frequently lacking; in other words, there is wanting a judgment based on evidence which cannot be false.

In its harmful aspects, fear frequently produces depression, sluggishness, and reduces vitality. Fear may be accompanied by and display abnormal emotional effects; for example, the imagination may be unduly aroused; sensory impressions may be misinterpreted and exaggerated; attention may be directed to insignificant details, and frequently diverted from factors and causes of major concern; and the power to reason logically and judge correctly may be temporarily lessened, so that the exercise of self-control is somewhat impaired or even rendered impossible. Thus, fear may exert a paralyzing influence on human conduct, and its consequences can be far reaching because the individual's conduct may be motivated by emotion rather than by reason. When conduct is ruled by emotion one finds it difficult to face reality and to form right attitudes toward those objects which arouse the emotions. It goes without saying that every effort should be made to avoid these undesirable effects of fear. Through proper educational training and guidance, one should learn the true meaning of fear and how to control it intelligently, and thereby acquire that *spiritual poise* implied in "freedom from fear."

In its salutary aspects, fear may take the following forms: fear of the judgment and wrath of God in consequence of evil acts; fear of the consequent punishment when lawfully constituted authority, either civil or religious, is disobeyed; fear of losing one's physical and mental health because of neglect, indifference, sin, or ignorance. Freedom from fear can never rightly mean the elimination or even the studied disregard of these salutary aspects. This is evident from the fact that these very aspects form an integral part of man's nature and purpose, and serve to govern his quest for ultimate happiness. They provide sanctions, moreover, to control individual and social conduct, because fear of punishment and fear of the loss of God's grace and blessing serve as most powerful deterrents against evil.

Monsignor Fulton J. Sheen describes in cogent terms the most important salutary aspect of fear as follows:

I say, fear Him, not as we fear evil, but fear Him as we fear losing what we love. The more we love anyone the greater is our fear lest misfortune or death steal that person away. So with ourselves; our love of God as a nation must begin with "fear," for the "fear of God is the beginning of all wisdom": first the fear of the sanctions of His Justice, then the fear of betraying the blessings of Mercy. God is no tyrant waiting to catch us in our misdemeanors; if He were He should have blotted us all out of existence centuries ago. But He is Divine Justice and as such we cannot expect to rebel against His love or escape the consequences for "by whatsoever a man sinneth, so also shall he be punished." The law of God is not arbitrary or external but just and inexorable, for the wages of sin is death. Once we recognize this Justice, we prepare ourselves for that holier fear — the fear of hurting the thing we love, which makes us cry out with the publican: "Lord, be merciful unto me a sinner."[12]

Certain fears which the Fourth Freedom seeks to eradicate, and thereby promote the common good of man, are: fear of unjust aggression from one's neighbor, enemy, or state; fear of bodily harm or moral corruption to oneself, one's family, and one's nation; fear lest opportunities be absent or denied to earn a living wage, to maintain a normal standard of living, and to be secure in one's rights, property, and possessions against unlawful usurpation on the part of some external authority. To the end that these fears may be overcome, "freedom from fear" ought to promote man's security by providing a firm political, economic, social, and moral foundation for a new world order based on truth and justice, which will preclude any threat to the exercise of legitimate individual rights and the discharge of personal obligations.

Freedom from fear, then, in its correct meaning, implies the necessary protection and guarantee that there will be no unjust aggression whereby one's person, domestic peace, family stability, security in possession of one's rightful property, will be threatened. It includes, moreover, liberty to order one's life in such way that one is "master of his fate and captain of his

---

[12] Sheen, F. J., *A Declaration of Dependence* (Milwaukee: The Bruce Publishing Co., 1941), pp. 117–118.

soul." In his own way and by virtue of his own talents, subject duly to authority, man can thus strive to overcome the unnecessary fears that continually beset him, and live in peace with his God, with his neighbor, and with himself. Freedom from fear implies, furthermore, the safeguarding of those agencies which cooperate in the promotion of the material and spiritual welfare of the individual and society, namely, the family, the Church, and the State. When this latter security is provided for, the common good is advanced and the freedom of man is enlarged, politically, socially, economically, and morally. President Roosevelt refers to this "security" in the following manner:

Let us remember that economic safety for the America of the future is threatened unless a greater economic stability comes to the rest of the world. We cannot make America an island in either a military or an economic sense. Hitlerism, like any other form of crime or disease, can grow from the evil seeds of economic as well as military feudalism.

Victory in this war is the first and greatest goal before us. Victory in the peace is the next. That means striving toward the enlargement of the security of man here and throughout the world — and, finally, striving for the "fourth freedom" — freedom from fear.[13]

When the foregoing interpretations of freedom and the Four Freedoms are understood, accepted, and applied in every expression of individual and social action, then it can rightly be said that the democratic way of life becomes a reality, and that "all men's good" becomes "each man's rule." This way of life can be achieved only by a persevering struggle of every

---

[13] *Congressional Record,* Vol. 89, No. 2, January 7, 1943, p. 48.

right thinking individual against the forces of evil and destruction. Groundless optimism resulting from military successes or underestimation of the magnitude of the task must be overcome. The road to final victory through the Four Freedoms is long and hard. Delays must be expected and provided for; they should serve to stimulate even greater efforts toward the ultimate success of the democratic way of life. This way of life is truly the Christian way of life, which, as the following chapter will show, has its bases in the firm foundations of truths divinely revealed for man's guidance and accepted by true philosophy, to the end that every man may attain his proper material and spiritual purposes consonant with his true nature and the correct functions of society.

Chapter II

THE BASES OF THE FOUR FREEDOMS

INTRODUCTION. In the foregoing chapter, the meaning and necessary limitations of freedom and the Four Freedoms were set forth. It was shown that freedom, although an inalienable right of man, bestowed on him as a gift by his Creator, must be exercised according to its proper meaning and within its legitimate boundaries. It was pointed out, furthermore, that freedom has a moral foundation; that its right exercise is dependent on conformity to law, divine and human; and, finally, that such conformity offers the strongest guarantee for promoting the common good of society, as well as the immediate and ultimate good of the individual.

These questions now arise: Where are found the bases of the Four Freedoms, the fundamental truths in which they have their source? Are their bases found in science? in sociology? in economics? in the philosophies of naturalism, socialism, exaggerated nationalism, communism, or experimentalism? Or must they be sought, finally, in true philosophy and divinely revealed religion?

SCIENCE. Are the bases of the Four Freedoms found in science? The answer to this question lies, first of all, in an exact definition of science. Science means that systematized body of knowledge which describes and explains proximate causes. It comprises an orderly arrangement of truths concerning reality which have been discovered by observation, experimentation, and induction, and have been tested by repeated researches and validated by proper criteria. Science seeks to discover facts and to explain their immediate causes, and the principles and laws underlying these facts. In brief, then, science is nothing more than getting the facts, testing them, validating them, and finally, expounding them as truths by appropriate demonstration and explanation.

Broadly speaking, science embraces that knowledge which is derived from the investigation of all reality; that is, everything having existence: persons, being, material and immaterial objects, organic and inorganic matter, etc. In this broad sense, science may be said to fall logically into two categories: (1) *natural science,* the purpose of which is to attain specific knowledge of material things, their proximate causes and immediate purposes and functions; (2) *speculative science* or *philosophy,* the scope of which includes the truths derived from reason and revelation, and which provides the interpretation of ultimate causes, i.e., the answer to the last *what, why, Who.*

Strictly considered, however, the term "science" is limited to an explanation of material things and their immediate causes, effects, and applications. In this strict meaning, science comprises the sum total of various organized bodies of truths which have been grouped according to a particular plan for study, and each of these bodies is described as "a science," a special branch of study. These particular branches are called pure or applied sciences. Thus, biology, astronomy, botany, chemistry, geology, and zoology are said to be pure sciences. Each comprises a body of knowledge related to a particular field of study. Again, engineering, medicine, agronomy, mechanics, navigation are applied sciences. The basic principles or laws of these applied sciences flow from those pure sciences to which they are related.

It is assumed by many that science, through use of the experimental or, as it is usually called, the scientific method, can supply all the knowledge required by man to fulfill the needs of individual and social life. It is held, moreover, that knowledge is the outcome of free experiences which, when tested and approved by the scientific method, are to be accepted as verified truth. Science is said to be the tested thought products resulting from the experimental method. Any so-called "truth" or "knowledge" which cannot be established, verified, and applied by use of the experimental method is considered unknowable, unreal, and but a figment of the imagination.

Now, with all due respect to the legitimate place, contributions, and findings of science resulting from the correct use of the scientific method, it is clear that there are fundamental truths, aspects of reality, which science, of itself, cannot know or discover through the scientific method. These truths are knowable by man solely through reason and revelation, for they transcend the boundaries of overt human experience and the limits of the scientific experiment. Among these truths are: the existence and immortality of the soul, the freedom of the will, the moral law, man's divine creation, man's supernatural destiny, original sin, man's condition as a result of original sin, man's inalienable rights as free gifts from the Creator. Knowledge of these truths is essential, for only by a way of life founded and constructed upon them can man attain the end of his creation and discharge his individual and social obligations.

Within its own boundaries science represents the highest degree of probability that has been discovered to date. It is not, however, infallible in its teachings, but is subject, rather, to revealed truth. Science is limited by the relative imperfection of its instruments, the nature of certain experiments, and the scope of its legitimate province. It is subject, moreover, to the weaknesses, preconceptions, and prejudices of the human beings who make the observations, perform the experiments, and interpret the findings. No one is infallible, because, on account of original sin, each is subject to the characteristic limitations of an intellect less able than in the preternatural state to attain truth, a will less able to seek the good, and a nature more inclined to evil.

It is clear, then, that science, by its very definition, scope, and inherent limitations, cannot supply the bases of the Four Freedoms. These latter are founded, of necessity, on the following realities: the existence of God; the immortality of the soul; the freedom of the will; an unchanging moral law; a correct and complete interpretation of man's fallen but redeemed nature, and of his inalienable rights; a respect for and obedience to constituted authority, human and divine; the furtherance of the common good of society by the fostering of the individual's material and spiritual welfare. The omission of any one of the foregoing realities means inability to provide the bases of freedom and the Four Freedoms. Science includes within its legitimate scope only *one* of these necessary realities; namely, the promotion of the common good and the individual's material welfare. But it is on all these realities that the bases of the Four Freedoms rest, because freedom has essentially a spiritual and a moral foundation. Both its bases and its ultimate sanctions transcend quantitative, material realities, and hence are beyond the province of natural science.

SOCIOLOGY. Are the bases of the Four Freedoms found in sociology? The answer may be had from an examination of the meaning and scope of modern sociology. As was previously shown, the purpose of science is to obtain knowledge of facts, laws, principles, immediate causes and consequences, and to explain them. Now, science can be divided according to the object which it treats and the data related thereto: for example, natural science, biological science, psychological science, speculative science, theological science, and social science. When the efforts of science are directed to the study of man and his life, an important body of data is accumulated, and constitutes what is commonly described as social science. Thus, social science embraces the sum of those particular fields of knowledge, termed social sciences, which are concerned exclusively with some aspect of society, or man's social life, such as, social amelioration, political science, economics, social ethics, social hygiene and sanitation. One of the social sciences is the study of society itself, termed sociology.

Sociology may be defined as that social science which

is concerned exclusively with human society: its origin, nature, evolution, constitution, and with man's place and purpose in society. Its subject matter comprises the study of society, social origins, social culture, social institutions, social interstimulation, social competition, social conflict, social interaction, social amelioration, in fine, every aspect of cooperative group life. By society is meant the state of living in association with one's fellow man for the purpose of "harmonious coexistence," and the attainment of mutual benefits thereby for all. Society is, in fact, the aggregate of persons living in a well-organized community and cooperating for the improvement of the social order. Society possesses certain well-defined characteristics or elements, namely, plurality of individuals, community of purposes, collective action for the mutual welfare of all, and constituted authority. It should be recognized that possession of these common elements does not necessarily imply the promotion of the common good, because it is possible to have a society, in the correct meaning of the term, whose object is fundamentally bad, such as a society of pirates organized solely for plunder and depredation.

Sociology seeks to understand and interpret social phenomena, and thus promote man's individual, temporal welfare as well as the welfare of society as a whole. It studies man as a social animal existing for a social purpose; and under many modern interpretations, it has a social end, namely, the service of society. Sociology supplies facts concerning the environment which are said to affect and condition the individual in his every act and to direct his forces and purposes to the attainment of social ends. Thus, the individual's development and material welfare are made dependent on society; and sociology seeks to formulate hypotheses, theories, principles, and laws, which will interpret and govern all social progress. Its methods are largely those of observation and induction, but of late years they have included the so-called "scientific" or "experimental" method of science. A purposeful attempt is made, at present, to apply this method to the scientific study of society, to the end that social controls may be made effective, that social reconstruction may follow predetermined experimentalist notions of progress, and that the ideal society of the future may be effectively conditioned and forged into a reality.

Modern sociology, outside the Catholic interpretation of the field, follows the purpose and course set by its founder, Auguste Comte, a positivist, and further pursued in England by Spencer, and in America by later exponents such as Ward, Small, Sumner, Giddings, Ogburn, Keller, etc. It has remained true to its original form because it is still essentially positivistic. Its data are drawn exclusively from empirical sources of knowledge, and are interpreted according to materialistic norms. Knowledge derived from rational sources and from an infallible source, namely, divine revelation, is excluded.

It can be seen quite readily from an examination of the modern meaning and positivistic trend of sociology, that its concern is primarily and exclusively with the control and effective conditioning of society, its institutions, and all its ramifications, to the end that society will be reconstructed according to a particular pattern. This pattern is predetermined to emphasize that man is a creature of society and exists solely to promote social ends and purposes. When society so conceived progresses, then also is man's material welfare promoted. Because of its positivistic and exclusively materialistic interpretation of man, his purposes and final end, sociology can never supply the bases of the Four Freedoms. Man's exercise and enjoyment of these freedoms, not only in his interior life but in his social life as well, must at all times be governed by eternal verities and sanctions which transcend social forces and controls. Man's inalienable rights, being gifts from his Creator, can never be interpreted, limited or ruled solely by social forces, or be founded on materialistic, positivistic norms. The bases of the Four Freedoms, therefore, cannot be found in sociology.

ECONOMICS. Are the bases of the Four Freedoms to be sought in economics? An examination of the purpose and meaning of this social science will provide the answer. Not a few modern thinkers assert that the peoples of the world are bound together inseparably only by "an economic world union," and, hence, that the bases of the Four Freedoms are found exclusively in economics. Such thinkers hold that there is an "economic unification of mankind"; that the "debt and credit system" is the root of all civilization and explains its present organization; and that this system must serve to control all future development of civilization toward the effecting of world peace and the exercise of the Four Freedoms. In other words, the peoples of the world are bound together mainly by economic relationships, and the solution of present-day problems must recognize the economic interdependence and the economic unity of all peoples. Thus Scherman writes:

An economic and cultural world-union is in existence. That great fact must determine the nature of the peace-effort. This unification is growing closer and more intricate with every year. It must be matched by a world political organization which *limits the sovereignty* of each and every nation, wherever the exercise of that sovereignty irresponsibly takes no account of the economic interests of all the unified peoples.[1]

From the moment when God enjoined man with these words, "In the sweat of thy face shalt thou eat bread, till thou return to the earth . . ." (Gen. 3:19), one of the major concerns of mankind has been the satisfaction of physical needs. St. Thomas points out that two things are necessary for man's well-being: to act virtuously, and to possess a sufficiency of material goods necessary for the exercise of virtue.[2] Man seeks, therefore, to acquire for himself and others a sufficiency of these goods. This sufficiency is commonly described as wealth, or the material means of satisfying human wants and desires, and is termed the science of economics. Economics may be defined in a particular sense, then, as that social science which concerns the business of earning one's living. Its content embraces the laws and facts governing the production, distribution, and consumption of wealth. It studies the material means of meeting man's physical wants and providing for them. In a wider sense, economics implies the use of the resources of the community for the purpose of effecting orderly conduct and productivity, to the end that material prosperity may be increased and man's wants thereby may receive maximum satisfaction.

---

[1] Scherman, H., *The Last Best Hope of Earth* (New York: Random House, 1941), pp. 39–40.
[2] Cf. Chapter I, pp. 27–28.

Economics, then, as a social science seeks the most complete and effective body of knowledge concerning the production, distribution, and consumption of the increments derived from land, labor, and capital, so that man's material wants may be satisfied in conformity with the economic laws governing supply, demand, utility, and value. Thus, economics is concerned exclusively with man's material welfare, which, in turn, has applications to his social well-being and spiritual destiny. These latter, however, do not come within the scope of economics as that science is commonly known outside the Catholic sphere.

While economics contributes immeasurably to the organization of an appropriate world order in which the Four Freedoms may be enhanced, yet, of itself, economics cannot supply the bases of these freedoms. As a social science, it is limited exclusively to a particular aspect of social life, namely, the business of earning a living in order to satisfy material wants. Man's material well-being alone does not constitute all that is required for the fulfillment of his purposes, because "man liveth not by bread alone, but by every word of God" (Luke 4:4). Even when it is rightly interpreted as limited to the production, distribution, and consumption of wealth, economics still is constrained within the scope of satisfying man's material wants. Freedom and the Four Freedoms can be had only when *all* man's wants, physical, social, intellectual, moral, aesthetic, and spiritual, are provided. The bases of the Four Freedoms, then, cannot be supplied by economics.

MATERIALISTIC PHILOSOPHIES. It is clear, so far, that the bases of the Four Freedoms cannot be found in science, sociology, or economics. Are they to be found, then, in the philosophies of naturalism, socialism, exaggerated nationalism, communism, or experimentalism? Since all of these are materialistic philosophies of life, it is essential that the meaning of materialism be set forth.

Materialism means that all reality is attributable to the dynamic operation of matter, the blind forces of which account for its varied transformation and development. It stresses the all-sufficiency of matter as explanatory of every aspect of reality. Materialism denies the existence of the soul, and the existence of any spiritual being which might be asserted in explanation of, or as governing, reality. No recognition is given to any values or sources of authority except those immanent in matter. The true worth and dignity of human personality are completely misinterpreted by those who hold that man exists solely as a form of matter for the service of matter. Thus, man must serve nature, society, the State, the community, all of which are held to be an extension of matter. Man's place in the scheme of things is constructed on purely pragmatic norms and on an unyielding fatalism that emphasizes his final end as the grave. According to materialism, man originated in matter and will return to matter.

In the twentieth century, various forms of materialism have attained significant proportions, and have lately presented varied interpretations of man, reality, society, morality, freedom. Each of these interpretations, however, is postulated on the all-sufficiency of matter as the source of values and authority; and each constitutes an exclusive philosophy of life, which counts within its ranks numerous exponents and followers not only in the United States but also in the world at large. Five of these philosophies, namely, naturalism, socialism, exaggerated nationalism, communism, and experimentalism, will now be examined to discover whether or not the bases of the Four Freedoms are found therein. The answer to this question can be had from an examination of the meaning and tenets of each of these philosophies.

1. NATURALISM. Many definitions of naturalism have been formulated. In the majority of them is found the basic notion that naturalism excludes any spiritual or supernatural interpretation of the origin and end of man and the world. Naturalism depends solely on natural causes to explain and to solve all philosophical and social problems. A workable definition of naturalism may be stated as follows: Naturalism is that doctrine which asserts that man, his world, and his manner of living, are to be explained without any reference to the supernatural, because man is a product of and continuous with nature.

TENETS OF NATURALISM. While the adherents of naturalism disagree as to exact definition, they seem to agree on each of the following tenets: (1) Everything that exists has its origin in nature and must be explained by nature's laws. (2) Physical nature is the central element around which revolves all reality. (3) Man lives for this world alone and must, at all times and in all things, conform to nature's laws. (4) Man, society, all that exists, are merely the results of the "blind forces" of nature "acting upon matter."

MODERN FORMS OF NATURALISM. It should be made clear that naturalism is not a wholly separate and distinct system of philosophy. It is, in part, dependent on and related to materialism, and has influenced the development of socialism, exaggerated nationalism, communism, and experimentalism. From its relationship to other philosophies naturalism has assumed several forms, which for ease of interpretation and in order to discover whether or not the bases of the Four Freedoms are found therein, may be treated under three divisions:

1) The first is usually described as *biological naturalism*. This form asserts that the only sources whence man may obtain knowledge with any degree of certainty concerning his origin, nature, and destiny, are the natural sciences, especially the science of biology. According to biological naturalism, man's origin, development, and life in society, as well as his freedom, are explained and controlled solely by the biological laws of nature. The exercise and enjoyment of freedom, then, is not based on an inalienable right of man, but rather on the beneficence of nature and is sanctioned only by nature's laws.

2) The second form is termed *psychological naturalism*. Its advocates seek to make psychology, instead of philosophy, interpretative of human conduct and social life, based always, of course, on nature's laws. According to this type, all human behavior is interpreted on a purely psychological and mechanistic basis. By the use of appropriate stimuli, conduct can be conditioned and the individual made to conform to his role of "continuity with nature." The spirituality of intellect and will is denied. Intelligence is said to be merely the result of the operation of the brain, a manifestation of the activity of cortical neurons. The power of will is interpreted as a mere response which is evoked and determined by the pleasure-pain factor. Indeed, it is

through psychological naturalism that modern non-Catholic psychology has been transformed into a mechanistic psychology which has become essentially behavioristic, by reason of its emphasis on the all-important process of conditioning. Freedom itself, therefore, as well as the exercise and enjoyment of the Four Freedoms, is interpreted as a mere product of evolutionary development and is limited to whatever standard is set by social approval in a changing social order.

3) A third form is called *sociological naturalism*. This type seeks to apply the laws of nature to the direction and control of social life. Society is the ultimate reality, and the furtherance of the welfare of society is made the main purpose of man. Thus, sociology is held to be the most important source of knowledge for the study and interpretation of man, nature, and society. In this interpretation, the fundamental truths of philosophy are ignored, and freedom is made subject to and governed by the will of society.

NATURALISM AND THE FOUR FREEDOMS. The naturalistic concept of freedom holds that man, a creature of nature, is bound solely by nature's laws, and exists in a free environment independent of any authority except that imposed on him by nature itself. This same man, says the naturalist, should follow the bent and impulses of his own undisciplined and uncontrolled nature, because these impulses are nothing more than nature's laws in operation. It is clear, then, that, according to naturalism, self-expression, self-discovery, constitute freedom as well as the means for the exercise of the Four Freedoms.

Naturalism is false for the following reasons: (1) supernatural truths and religion are denied; (2) the value

of prayer, grace, the sacraments is negated; (3) naturalism completely misinterprets man's true nature by
its denial of original sin; (4) natural science is made
the source of all truth; (5) the scientific method is held
to be the sole method of studying man, and, therefore,
naturalism ignores ultimate truths of a supernatural
order which are essential to a correct view of man, his
nature, and final destiny; (6) naturalism seeks to eliminate the authority of the mature mind over the immature which is essential to man himself and to the
true concept of education; (7) by limiting life and its
pursuits to wholly materialistic aims and ends, the very
essence of freedom is destroyed because opportunity
is denied man, thereby, to dedicate his life to the ultimate purpose of his creation.

Naturalism cannot offer any reasonable basis on
which man's inalienable rights can rest, because it excludes the very truths on which these rights are founded.
It follows, then, that freedom, in the naturalistic sense,
can never become a reality in the true meaning of that
term, and, hence, that the Four Freedoms, in their full
and correct expression, are rendered impossible. Thus,
freedom of speech and expression under naturalism
means to say and to do what one wills, for by so doing
one conforms to nature's laws. Freedom of religion implies the worship of the blind forces immanent in
nature, and evidenced by the operation of nature's
biologic and economic laws. Freedom from want consists in, and is conditioned by, the pursuit and satisfaction of man's desires, unhindered by authority or by
the unchanging injunctions of morality. Freedom from
fear means the necessity for man to make essential adjustments to nature's laws, and thereby avoid the retri-

bution, real or simulated, which follows disconformity
to the requirements placed on him by virtue of his
"continuity with nature."

It is evident, then, that the Four Freedoms are distorted and frustrated by these exclusive naturalistic
interpretations. The obvious reason for this is that
naturalism denies all eternal verities, teaches that everything is in a state of flux, and that constant change
characterizes nature. Freedom is said to change in its
mode of expression and is subject to the accidental
conditions of environment, rather than to the unchanging principles of the eternal law. Hence, under naturalism, what might be considered as an expression
of the Four Freedoms in one locality might be denied
and excluded in another. Thus, true freedom, which
has a moral foundation essentially, and, hence is applicable to all persons everywhere in the world, is
denied. It should be concluded, then, that the bases of
the Four Freedoms cannot be found in the false, exclusive philosophy of naturalism.

2. SOCIALISM. Socialism may be defined as that philosophy of life which teaches that society is the source
and end of man and all reality, and that all values are
measured in terms of contributions to social progress. According to this philosophy, social interests must
always take precedence over individual purposes, desires, and ends. Man is said to be a product of society,
of the group, and exists solely to serve and promote
the interests of the group. To naturalism, man is a
human animal; to socialism, he is a social animal. All
values are determined by society. Thus, according to
socialism, religion and morality are products of social
life, and since society is constantly changing, religion

and morality also must change and be determined by pragmatic values. All authority comes from the group, and claims to authority from any source other than society are vigorously denied.

TENETS OF SOCIALISM. According to socialism, man is man because he is a social animal. This is borne out by the following main tenets of socialism: (1) The individual is a member of society and must submit to its sanctions. (2) Society supplies all the means necessary for man's development and socialization. (3) Society is the great reality; it alone is self-perpetuating and permanent. (4) The individual is a product of society because all his conduct and creative activity are made possible and controlled by society. (5) All personal interests must be subordinated to group interests. (6) Society determines right and wrong, and sets up institutions designed to promote "the greatest good of the greatest number." (7) Sociology supplies all the knowledge needed for efficient, cooperative social life.

SOCIALISM AND THE FOUR FREEDOMS. From an analysis of the meaning and tenets of socialism it is clear that this is a false philosophy of life. It is false because socialism presents an erroneous interpretation of society and of the individual, who is the constituent unit of society. Socialism is exclusive because it sets up society as the great reality, and seeks to make religion, morality, as well as ethics, the products of society. Thus, human reason, and divine revelation are excluded as sources of knowledge capable of governing and directing man's conduct. By such exclusion, all authority is held to be resident in society, and, therefore, in effect, the authority of God, of the moral law, and of the family is denied. Since socialism vests all authority in society, which exists solely on a materialistic plane, and, hence, denies the authority of God, it is clear that there can be no true and complete interpretation of freedom under socialism. Freedom itself is a gift to man from God; it has, therefore, a moral foundation. It reaches its acme when the individual accepts and submits to divine authority. In place of this authority, socialism seeks to substitute *itself*.

It should be remembered that society, in its correct and exact meaning, is the aggregate of individuals grouped together for the purpose of achieving common material and spiritual objectives through the medium of cooperative efforts. The goal of society is the promotion of the immediate and ultimate good of each and every individual. While it is true, in certain instances, that the good of the individual must sometimes be subordinated to the common good of all, yet, the common good at all times and in all its aspects must be conformed to God's laws, to man's rational nature and last end, and must serve to facilitate the attainment of that end. It is plain that socialism is a false and exclusive philosophy because it denies to man any end or purpose other than society itself.

Sound reasoning will quickly convince one that the individual cannot be absorbed by the group, and that his final end and spiritual aspirations cannot be dictated exclusively by society. That end and those aspirations transcend the scope of material reality, and are governed by the eternal law and the truths of divine revelation. The individual is not exclusively a product of society nor does society grant him his inalienable rights, one of which is freedom. This latter is distinctly a gift from man's Creator, which cannot be taken away or usurped. Since God created man, all that man has, his intellect and his will, his talents, his capacity for creative achievement, and his pursuit of vocational interests, is made possible by the endowment given him by his Creator. Were it not for his intellect and will, the individual would be reduced to the level of the animal and be entirely incapable of creative productivity through his own efforts, or of profiting from the experiences of others. It is because of his intellect and free will that man can know and choose to do what is right and good in conformity to his rational nature, and thus exercise and enjoy the Four Freedoms to their full measure.

Socialism is in gross error when it seeks to subordinate all personal interests and human strivings to those of the group, for the reason that man, by his very nature, has specific duties to discharge not only to his fellow men, but to his Creator and to himself. These cannot with justice be subordinated to society alone, nor can they be made to subserve the whims and fancies of any social situation, institution, social end, or group desire. Society cannot determine what is right and wrong merely on the basis of what may be beneficial or harmful to the common good of society. On the contrary, right and wrong are determined objectively by the unchanging principles of the eternal law of God, which is applicable to all men everywhere in the world, and admits of no subjective modification. What society may hold to be the "greatest good of the greatest number" may be in reality a denial of the eternal law, may constitute a debasement of man's purposes, and may well be a violation of man's rational nature as well as of his inalienable rights.

According to socialism, freedom has its meaning and

its mode of expression entirely in society. Freedom of speech and expression means that man must say and do only what society permits him to say and do. Since society changes, and social forces are constantly seeking to effect new adjustments to changed conditions, freedom, likewise, must be governed by change and adjustment. Society, then, may exclude, deny, or limit at its will the expression and enjoyment of freedom. It is patent that this God-given, inalienable right can never be subjected to the accidental fancies and interpretations of a purely materialistic social order. Rather, the full meaning and expression of freedom must, perforce, be founded on and conformed to eternal moral standards, which truly dignify man's nature, interpret his rights, and aid the attainment of both his mundane and his supernatural destiny.

Freedom of religion under socialism implies that man, in so far as the spiritual aspirations of his nature are concerned, must bow before the golden calf of social materialism, because religion and morality are said to be exclusively the product of society. In the final analysis, therefore, God and society are considered one and the same. Thus, in the exercise of freedom under socialism, man's intellect and will are frustrated in their search for their respective formal objects, namely, truth and goodness. In place of these formal objects are substituted socialistic "truth," social goodness, and social ideals, which must be accepted without question.

Freedom from want, according to socialism, means complete submission on the part of the individual to the will of society, and the acceptance of its paternalism and apparent benefits. This freedom is exercised to the full when man cooperates completely with his fellow men in the service of society, because society alone can satisfy all man's wants. When society promotes man's physical and social wants, then it brings about his freedom.

Freedom from fear, under socialism, is attained by complete conformity to the will and approved practices of the group, to the end that, as a result of this conformity, every activity of the individual may meet with social approval. Thus, freedom from fear implies absence of the social sanctions which follow social disapproval of conduct.

It should be concluded that socialism, like its progenitor naturalism, is a false philosophy of life and, as such, presents an erroneous interpretation of freedom in general and of the Four Freedoms in particular. True freedom has a moral foundation, and must, at all times, represent man's capacity to choose what is right and good in harmony with his rational nature. Socialism denies not only the true origin of freedom, but also man's obligation to act according to his rational nature. Such a philosophy by its very exclusivism cannot, therefore, supply the bases of the Four Freedoms.

3. NATIONALISM. Despite various differences as to the meaning of nationalism, this basic notion seems to flow through every interpretation, namely, that all individual and group efforts are to be directed to the furtherance of national interests, purposes, and ideals, to the end that national culture may be perpetuated and national prosperity promoted to the maximum degree. It is clear, then, that the means employed to further particular nationalistic ideals, to promote national prosperity, and the spirit with which these are pursued may represent either an acceptable or an ex-

aggerated form of nationalism. In the acceptable form, the true nature, purpose, and end of the individual are recognized. Care is taken, moreover, to foster and provide for his material and spiritual development, and at the same time to promote the welfare of the nation, consonant with objective moral standards. Exaggerated nationalism, on the other hand, asserts complete authority by the nation or State over the individual in every aspect of his life. Whereas naturalism makes man a product of nature, and socialism makes him a product of society, exaggerated nationalism considers him a product of the nation or State. It holds that the individual exists solely to serve the nation and to promote its material welfare. All that the individual is, and hopes to be, are due to the beneficence of his nation. In other words, the nation is man's origin and final end. It is this form of nationalism, exaggerated, that is now under examination to determine whether or not nationalism, as so considered, can supply the bases of the Four Freedoms.

TENETS OF EXAGGERATED NATIONALISM. The basic principles of exaggerated nationalism are drawn from certain theories which stress race, geographical position, language, and a particular culture. The tenets of exaggerated nationalism which are drawn from such theories are as follows: (1) Man is born into the nation and exists solely to serve its interest. (2) The nation supplies all the means necessary for man's development and complete nationalization. (3) The individual is a product of the nation, and, therefore, all his activities come under its supervision and control. (4) All personal interests must be sacrificed to national interests. (5) The nation determines what is right and what is wrong, and the individual must submit unhesitatingly to "national truth." (6) The nation is the origin of all authority, rights, and duties.

The foregoing tenets of exaggerated nationalism have as their purpose the complete interpretation and domination of man, religion, morality, and social life. They regulate the political, social, and economic advancement of the nation. This advancement is achieved by the effective control of all natural resources, man power, and even the scope and exercise of freedom itself. Because exaggerated nationalism holds that the nation is the source of all authority, and that only its sanctions are binding on all its members, the *supernatural* source of authority and the moral foundation of the Four Freedoms are denied.

EXAGGERATED NATIONALISM AND THE FOUR FREEDOMS. From a study of the meaning and tenets of exaggerated nationalism, the conclusion should readily be drawn that it is a false philosophy of life. It is false because it erroneously interprets reality, the legitimate scope and function of the nation, and the origin, nature, and end of man.

Exaggerated nationalism misinterprets reality when it holds that everything that exists is in some way a product of national life, and must subserve the nation. It misinterprets the legitimate scope and function of the nation by its regimentation of the individual and the attempted usurpation of the rights of the family and the Church. Finally, it misinterprets the origin, nature, and end of man because it negates his divine creation, his fall and redemption, and his spiritual inheritance. The nation is not the source of man's inalienable rights, nor can it with justice attempt to regiment their legitimate exercise and expression. Freedom is one of man's inalienable rights, and, despite all physical regimentation by exaggerated nationalism, it has always a moral foundation. Hence, it can never truly be interpreted by purely materialistic, nationalistic norms.

It is true that man has certain obligations to his nation, which ought to be discharged with devotion, zeal, and completeness. He has, however, obligations first of all to his Creator. The discharge of these primary obligations is requisite for the attainment of his eternal salvation. Man was created by God, not by the nation or State. The nation cannot determine what is right and wrong merely on the basis of national expediency. Right and wrong are governed by the eternal law of God, which is known to man by reason and revelation. In no way may it be said that "might makes right" or "all justice is political," because, on the contrary, justice and goodness are determined by the unchanging principles of the eternal law.

In exaggerated nationalism, freedom is either entirely denied or else so rigidly controlled that its exercise conforms exclusively to nationalistic patterns and purposes.

Freedom of speech and expression, under exaggerated nationalism, means merely the permission to say and do what the national leaders want said and done. The exercise of this freedom must, perforce, be rigidly controlled and restricted by careful censorship or employed for propaganda purposes, because free speech and expression, in their true and full meaning, would be opposed to the regimentation and practices employed by exaggerated nationalism to force its especial ideology on its citizens.

Freedom to worship God means, in reality, the worship of one's country, nation, or State, for these are considered by nationalism as synonymous with the term "God." Since the individual is said to be the product of his nation, to which he owes his very existence and development, then, his only duty is to serve his nation. Thus, to this worship of "nation," freedom of religion is largely restricted by exaggerated nationalism, and every individual interest, ambition, and personal want must be subordinated to the pursuit and worship of national progress.

Freedom from want, under exaggerated nationalism, means that the individual, when he submits completely to the national will, and devotes his entire life to the service of national ideals, will derive for himself the maximum of satisfaction for his material and physical needs. The reason is that the nation is held to be the creator of all things and the dispenser of all economic goods. The interpretation of wants, therefore, is limited to the physical and the economic. No recognition is given to the spiritual or moral wants of man, because these are unrecognized and even positively denied.

Freedom from fear means complete submission to national policies and practices, because, it is said, the nation alone guarantees and provides that material security and happiness which, by nature, man seeks and strives to attain. Under exaggerated nationalism, freedom from fear implies that the individual subordinate himself, his interests, and ambitions entirely to the nation, for in the nation alone are resident the power and the sanctions to provide this freedom.

It is evident from this brief discussion of exaggerated nationalism, its tenets, and its interpretation of the

Four Freedoms, that these freedoms do not have their
bases in this false philosophy of life. It should not be
concluded, however, that these freedoms cannot exist
and be rightly interpreted under a true and acceptable
form of nationalism. The latter is founded on fundamentally true principles and possesses, thereby, the
conditions under which the Four Freedoms may flourish
so that man's eternal destiny takes precedence over
national ends and purposes. However, it must be stated
that the bases of the Four Freedoms are not found in
the false philosophy of exaggerated nationalism.

4. COMMUNISM. Communism may be defined as that
materialistic philosophy of life which seeks, by world
revolution, the establishment of a dictatorship of the
proletariat in order to produce a classless society. The
chief aim of that classless society is a community of
property and an economic leveling, by which all persons are governed by this economic assumption, namely,
that "labor alone gives value." Government, society,
history, economic life, are interpreted as the result of
the blind evolution of matter, which is held to be
eternal. Thus, the existence of God, the soul, religion,
an objective code of morality is denied. Communism
seeks to control and pattern the social order according
to this materialistic world view.

Communism avers that "religion is the opium of the
people." Religion, according to communism, aids the
ruling class in exploitation of the poor, because it
keeps the latter in continuous subservience to the
former; hence, religion must be eradicated. While
"freedom of conscience," private belief, and religious
sentiment, are tolerated by Article 124 of the Soviet
Constitution, this tolerance is mainly theoretical and

for the sake of temporary expedience. When the dictatorship of the proletariat ends and communism is attained, then, all "freedom of conscience," private belief, and religious sentiment will necessarily vanish. Likewise, statal organization and instrumentality are to be employed as long as they aid in the transitional stage toward the attainment of a classless society; but when that final purpose has been reached, the State will, perforce, disappear. Communism disclaims in its final and perfected form the necessity for either religion or the State.

TENETS OF COMMUNISM. The following are the principal tenets of communism: (1) Matter is the source and explanation of all reality; hence, there are no spiritual values in either man or society — everything exists to promote the good of the proletariat. (2) All rights are resident in collective society; the individual has only duties to discharge toward this society. (3) The ideal society, namely, a classless society, is achieved through a process of economic leveling whereby all persons are rendered economically equal under the proletariat. To establish this classless society revolution is necessary, because only by revolution and violence can the ruling class be overthrown. (4) By the overthrow of bourgeois society the State will be abolished. When this is accomplished, a society known as the proletariat will be set up. This latter will be put under the administration of a temporary dictator, who is to serve until communism is fully achieved. (5) The sole purpose of the family is to supply new workers, new citizens, new soldiers. Marriage is regarded as a civil contract that can easily be broken by divorce. (6) Man and his environment are constantly changing because of economic

which is never

forces. (7) The community is the source of all authority; hence, the right of private ownership of productive property is denied. (8) The community exercises complete economic and juridical control over the individual.

The foregoing tenets are applied to the whole of reality. They interpret man, society, religion, authority, and morality. They are the very foundation for the exclusive and false concepts of freedom and the Four Freedoms which flow from the communistic philosophy of life. In the words of Pius XI:

> It (Communism) is a system full of errors and sophisms. It is in opposition both to reason and to divine revelation. It subverts the social order, because it means the destruction of its foundations; because it ignores the true origin and purpose of the State; because it denies the rights, dignity, and liberty of human personality.[3]

COMMUNISM AND THE FOUR FREEDOMS. From an examination of its meaning and tenets, it is clear that communism is a materialistic philosophy of life. Freedom, in the true meaning of the term, is thereby denied, because freedom itself must be founded on man's rational nature and his final end as governed by God's law. Since these latter are excluded, communism can supply sound foundations for neither freedom nor the proper exercise of the Four Freedoms.

By seeking to eliminate religion, communism arrogates to itself the right to effect a social order governed by the economic factor alone. Man is constrained to conform his conduct to decrees which are materialistic, collectivistic, and mandatory. He is no longer at liberty to accept that form of social order prescribed by

---

[3] Pius XI, *Divini Redemptoris, Social Wellsprings* (Milwaukee: The Bruce Publishing Co., 1942), Vol. II, p. 346.

divine law and founded on the immutable principles of truth, goodness, and charity.

It is evident to human reason that both man and society have their origin from God. They are mutually ordained, one to the other. Each has been given rights and obligations by the Creator. For the communist, however, society is a mere mechanical collectivity in which there are to be no classes, but rather a community of laborers, all equal and dedicated to the pursuit of a single cause, namely, the final perfection of communism, a classless society. Economic and legal control are exercised over the workers to the extent of regulating their every vocational pursuit and life activity. Thus, the inalienable right of the worker to choose his vocation and the manner in which he will live are denied. Likewise, the necessary obligation of civil society to foster and protect the temporal and *spiritual* welfare of its members is rejected.

For man's highest welfare, communism proclaims: "From each according to his ability, to each according to his need." But this is a purely materialistic, economic interpretation of needs, from which man's supernatural, intellectual, and moral needs are excluded. Hence, it is evident that no moral foundation for freedom can be found in the communist notion and plan of society.

Communism presents a false view of authority when it holds that the community alone is the source of all authority. In the words of Lenin: "The revolutionary dictatorship of the proletariat is an authority maintained by the proletariat by means of force over and against the bourgeoisie, and not bound by any laws."[4]

---

[4] Lenin, N., *The Proletarian Revolution* (London: The British Socialist Party, n.d.), p. 15.

Thus are denied the divinely constituted authority of the moral law, and the authority of parents derived from the natural law to rear their children in a holy and filial love and fear of God. On the basis of this communal authority, communism forbids private ownership of property. Such ownership, however, is one of man's natural rights. It indicates that one has what is *proper* to a person, that which he owns and over which he can exercise control. The right to property, then, is individual; its use is moral and social, and as such is determined by the common good, which good is subject at all times to the natural and divine law.

By affirming that morality is social in origin, constantly changing, and dependent on pragmatic norms, communism excludes one of the true foundations for freedom, namely, the moral law which is immutable and independent of man or society. There is denied, moreover, the fact that man's intellect seeks truth in its ultimate form; that his will seeks absolute goodness; and that his soul seeks eternal happiness for having lived "the good life" in conformity to the unchanging principles of God's laws. Right and wrong can never be known from the application of materialistic, social, and economic norms alone. Right and wrong are governed, fundamentally, by the moral law, and this law is applicable to every man in all his activities of whatever kind, individual, social, political, economic, and material. Communism, therefore, by its distortion of the meaning and application of religion and morality, violates man's rational nature and denies his inalienable rights.

Under communism, freedom means the power to do what the community insists the individual must do in order to share in the benefits of collective productivity. In other words, all freedom is resident in collectivity. Since communism assumes all authority, the exercise of freedom is limited by the degree to which it can serve the advancement of the proletariat. This limitation, therefore, is a form of economic security, a reward, as it were, for service to the collective group. Economic security is substituted for true freedom, which, in the correct meaning of the term, is a gift to man from his Creator. By placing freedom on a purely economic basis, communism denies the fundamentally moral foundation of freedom. Thus, under communism, man must choose to live and die for the ideology of the proletariat. His own personal rights, as well as his duties to himself, his fellow men, and his Creator, are denied. They are, likewise, prevented by the regimentation of the individual to the progressive attainment of communistic ideals. Freedom, then, is not regarded by communism as an inalienable right conferred on man as a gift by his Creator. Rather, it means to the communist mind certain liberties conferred on man as rewards for his complete submergence in the proletariat; and the continuance of these rewards or, as they are called, "securities," depends on his continued collective productivity, since labor alone is said to give value.

Freedom of speech and expression under communism means that the individual must say and do exactly and only what the proletariat permits. Thus, whatever is held best for the community justifies either the exercise or the limitation of this freedom. In the exercise of speech, then, propaganda may be spread, willful lies told, specious and deceptive arguments used, false claims presented, if these serve to promote the cause of communism. It is clear that freedom of speech and expression under communism have a pragmatic interpretation and, hence, that this freedom is subject to constant change, even to complete denial, if conditions warrant.

Freedom of religion, rightly interpreted, is positively denied by communism. While "private beliefs" and so-called "freedom of conscience" are permitted, these are tolerated only on the grounds of expediency. For the moment, religious tolerance may be "the party policy" as set forth in "the party line"; but all the specious rationalizations which this latter usually provides should be remembered. Although communism avers that "religion is the opium of the people," it holds also that in the process of transformation from the revolution to the termination of the dictatorship of the proletariat, the individual needs some of this "opium." When, however, the final state of communism is attained, atheism will prevail. Thus, freedom of religion, at best, means devotion to the cause of communism, which itself has assumed the character of a religion. Instead of presenting ultimate truth to man's intellect and goodness to his will, communism supplies proletarian truth and propaganda, and positively indoctrinates the individual in its materialistic ideology founded on the pragmatic norms of economic collectivism and dialectical materialism. This ideology is held to contain man's highest good.

Freedom from want means that "security" which comes when the individual gives to the community according to his capacity and receives from the community, in turn, according to his needs. Communism, of course, decides what is each person's capacity and what are his needs. No account is taken of man's moral and spiritual needs. In effect, communism positively prevents these needs from being adequately met. The exercise and enjoyment of freedom from want, therefore, is limited and dictated by this false materialistic philosophy of life, which prevents the individual's needs from receiving legitimate satisfaction.

Freedom from fear, in its right meaning, is impossible under communism, because such freedom is interpreted exclusively on a materialistic, economic, and social basis. As such, the true norms and sanctions of divine authority and the moral law are denied. These norms and sanctions are the very bulwark of this freedom, and without them it is impossible for man to pursue either his material or eternal happiness without fear of aggression from any source. Lack of security, lack of bread, are not man's only fears. The fears of "the inner man" are sometimes far more searching and compelling than are the fears that arise from lack of adequate economic subsistence and satisfaction.

The communistic concept, then, entails a false, exclusive, materialistic interpretation of the Four Freedoms. Man's inalienable rights and the very source of these rights, namely, God, are denied, as well as the moral law governing conduct. Because of this denial the expression of the Four Freedoms is either distorted or incomplete. Freedom has a moral foundation and implies man's capacity to choose and to do what is right according to his rational nature and the norms of morality, which exist outside of him. Because communism completely misinterprets man's rational nature, the norms of morality, and the sanctions of divine

authority, it cannot furnish the bases of the Four
Freedoms.

5. EXPERIMENTALISM. The advocates of this philosophy assert that it is "an indigenous American
philosophy"; that it alone is capable of interpreting democracy in the United States, and of directing its development through the reconstruction of the social
order.[5] Since the teachings of experimentalism are accepted unquestionably by numerous American educators, it is essential that this philosophy be critically
examined to determine whether or not a valid interpretation of freedom itself and, therefore, of the Four
Freedoms is presented.

MEANING OF EXPERIMENTALISM. There are three
basic teachings of experimentalism: (1) everything is
in a state of constant change; (2) thought and action are
inseparable; that is, each is held to be only a different
form of experience; (3) the democratic way of life and
the experimental way of life are one and the same.[6]

Kilpatrick describes experimentalism as follows:

Three conceptions seem to belong together here to make
up the experimentalist outlook: (1) the conception . . . that
ideas mean only their consequences in experience; (2) the
conception that experience, at least of the kind we are in-
terested in, is essentially social in origin and predominantly
social in purpose; and (3) the conception that we find out
what to expect in life by studying experimentally the uni-
formities within experience. If we put these three conceptions together we have a point of view at least promising
for the study of any and all human experience. If such a
method of attack should, as an hypothesis, not only explain

---

[5] Childs, J. L., *Education and the Philosophy of Experimentalism*
(New York: The Century Co., 1931), p. 229.
[6] "Progressive Education . . . Its Philosophy and Challenge," *Progressive Education*, Vol. 18, No. 5, May, 1941, Yearbook Supplement,
p. 12.

the already generally accepted positions in social-moral outlook, but also go on further to help us make advances in the study of philosophy and ethics and do these things better than do alternate proposals, then we can claim to have found a promising method of philosophizing. It is this outlook and method which is herein called *experimentalism.*[7]

In order to understand the meaning of experimentalism, one must be familiar with the specific views of this philosophy concerning the *world, man, morality, and democracy.*

1. THE WORLD. Man, says the experimentalist, lives in a world which is constantly changing; hence, everything (life, religion, morality, freedom) is subject to continuous change. There is no absolute, eternal truth. Truth is dependent upon and the result of a person's experience. What may be true for the individual today may not be true tomorrow. The only standard by which one can judge what is true is his own personal experience. Experience, then, is the only satisfactory means of judging the value of conduct, and of guiding man in his efforts to make those adjustments which are said to be necessary for his survival in a changing world. It may be readily seen that experimentalism bases its philosophy on human experience, and on what it calls "reconstructed experiences," as the only way by which one can discover knowledge. In other words, experimentalism holds that no one can attain certain knowledge except as a result of his own experience.

Since everything, according to experimentalism, is subject to change, experience also must be subject to

---

[7] *Forty-First Yearbook*, National Society for the Study of Education (Bloomington, Ill.: Public School Publishing Co., 1942), "Philosophies of Education," Part I, pp. 44–45.

change. Therefore, man must constantly reconstruct his experience in two different ways: (1) in making the needed adjustments to environment (a changing world); and (2) in modifying the environment, within certain limits, or in remaking the world according to a certain experimental pattern (reconstruction of experiences). The individual must make the necessary adjustments required by "the rapidly moving material aspects of our civilization," otherwise he cannot be free.

2. MAN. Experimentalism regards man as a wholly animal organism, a product of growth from lower forms of life, differing from other animals in *degree* but not in kind. Man is an end in himself, and exists solely for service to society. Man and his environment are not two separate things, but merely two aspects of one thing, because man is a part of nature and "continuous with nature." As a living organism, man's most distinguishing characteristic is his activity, his capacity to undergo a "humane experience."

The main difference between living and nonliving things, according to Dewey, one proponent of experimentalism, is that the activities of living things are characterized by efforts, needs, satisfactions, and purposeful responses. Thus, activity, intellect, thought, will, and feeling are inseparable; they are all forms of experience. In other words, "mind," the intellectual faculty, is not a separate and distinct power of the soul, but rather something which has developed in man, in the struggle for existence, as an instrument to aid him to reconstruct his experiences intelligently. Hence, "mind" is merely another term for activity. But, since man is a purposeful animal, he must act in such way as to reconstruct intelligently his past experiences, and direct and redirect his future activity to a specific immediate or remote objective. Thus, his behavior, since it leads to such a purposeful end, is said to be "intelligent behavior."

Experimentalism dispenses with the problem of how man gets his knowledge, asserting that "the world is subject matter for knowledge, because mind has developed in that world." It follows, therefore, that the experimentalist denies this fundamental truth concerning man's nature, namely, that "mind," "intelligence," and "will" are powers of the one, abiding, substantial, indivisible, spiritual principle in man, which is the soul. The experimentalist denies, moreover, that knowledge is acquired, truth and certitude obtained, only by virtue of the operation of the intellect in the normal fulfillment of its purpose, which is to ascertain truth. Furthermore, the experimentalist denies the fact that the will is a blind faculty which needs the light of the intellect to attain its proper object, which is the *good*. As pointed out, experimentalism teaches that thought, knowledge, will, mind, activity are merely forms of experience which can never be separated.

3. MORALITY. Experience, then, is made the sole criterion of truth and the only guide for moral conduct. Since, for the experimentalist, life is a constantly changing process, "a reconstruction of experience," and a redirection of activity through "anticipated sequences," it is clear that truth and morality must constantly change. On the basis that man, through experience, determines his own truth and, hence, his own morality, subject, of course, to social sanctions, experimentalism seeks to construct a "scientific morality" which excludes religion and is, therefore, independent of supernatural sanctions. This secular notion of moral-

ity requires new sources, standards, and sanctions. Its new sources are held to lie in the natural sciences. The standards of this morality are found in the continuous growth of experience. These sanctions are, of course, utilitarian, and are determined by social approval or disapproval.

It is quite evident that by this secular interpretation morality is placed on the level of the natural and physical sciences. Furthermore, Dewey emphasizes the point that moral theory, in its development and in the study thereof, must employ the same methods as the physical sciences.[8] The experimentalist notion of morality, which is the very basis of its "ethics" and its concept of freedom, holds that "growth through experience" is the ultimate or highest good. "Nothing is relative to growth save more growth," wrote Dewey. "The good" is to be found in those experiences which result from interaction between man and his environment. The test of good is experience, and its ultimate sanction is utility. From the viewpoint and teachings of experimentalism, there is no moral law outside of man, no decalogue binding in conscience. On the contrary, morality originates in human experience, and society fixes the standards and sanctions of that morality.

The fact that experimentalism makes experience the standard of morality has this implication: morality must always change because experience itself is in a state of constant change. Consequently, the experimentalist denies that there are objective, eternal standards on which to base morality and freedom, as well as their expression and enjoyment.

---

[8] Cf. Smith, M. J., *John Dewey and Moral Education* (Washington, D. C.: Guthrie Lithograph Co., 1939), Ch. X, p. 13.

In making mere social sanctions the only source of authority for man's actions, and the good of society the ultimate end of moral conduct, experimentalism reduces man to the status of a social instrument, the ultimate purpose of whose existence is solely the common social good. The individual's personal worth and dignity are fundamentally denied, because experimentalism rejects the truth that the worth and dignity of a human being lie in his moral nature, in his immortal soul, and in the ultimate end for which he was created, eternal happiness with his Creator.

4. DEMOCRACY. Democracy, according to the experimentalist, means the improvement of the common welfare, the greatest good of the greatest number, by the remaking and redirection of experiences wherein the individual takes part more and more actively in affairs of common or group interest. Since *everything* is in a state of continuous change, it is reasonable to suppose that democracy, likewise, is subject to change.

Democracy is an inclusive way of life which implies a continuous "reconstruction of beliefs and standards."[9] For the experimentalist, the democratic way of life has superseded religion. Democracy here on earth is the experimentalist substitute for the Christian heaven. By the application of the experimentalist method, ancient teachings and truths are dissolved and discarded. In their place, changing theories are set up which emphasize the individual's adjustment and readjustment of his own ideals and habits, by growth in and through experiences, so that his conduct may become responsive to new and ever changing conditions.

---

[9] Cf. Bode, B., *Democracy As a Way of Life* (New York: The Macmillan Co., 1937), p. 51.

As was brought out earlier in the discussion of the experimentalist view of man, the world, and morality, experience is the source of all knowledge, and knowledge cannot be separated from action. It follows, therefore, that the experimentalist arrives at the knowledge of democracy and its meaning solely through the medium of experience, and the reconstruction of experience. The ancient teaching of true philosophy concerning democracy, namely, that democracy receives its life, its purpose, and its spiritual force from religion, because all the rights implied in true democracy come from God, is replaced by a new notion; a notion that denies God as Creator, rejects the necessity of religion, and asserts that man can remake his world and "mold it nearer to the heart's desire" through the constant reconstruction of his own experiences.

Through the medium of progressive education, the experimentalist seeks to implement democracy, and to transform the social order according to his exclusive philosophy and his particular pattern of life. In short, the experimentalist's concept of democracy embraces the building of a new social order, a collectivistic order indeed, through the constant reconstruction of group experiences.

TENETS OF EXPERIMENTALISM. Briefly, then, the following are the major tenets of experimentalism: (1) Everything in the world is subject to continuous change. (2) Man is a higher animal, a product of chance, differing in degree but not in kind from the lower animals. (3) The only source of knowledge is experience; knowledge and action are inseparable. (4) Through experience, man creates his own values, his own truth, his own concept of freedom, and in this way is capable of remaking the social order. (5) Morality has its source only in experience; the sanctions of morality lie in the will of society. (6) Intelligence is a form of experience, a tool by which behavior is stimulated and guided by anticipated desirable consequences for the purpose of remaking experience. (7) Freedom is something acquired by man through the continuous "reconstruction of experience," in which the individual is the end and society the means. (8) Democracy is an "inclusive way of life" which entails a constant "reconstruction of beliefs and standards."

These tenets interpret the whole of reality, and from them flows the particular notion of freedom held by experimentalism.

EXPERIMENTALISM AND THE FOUR FREEDOMS. It is evident from its meaning and tenets that experimentalism is a materialistic philosophy of life. It presents exclusive interpretations of the world, man, morality, democracy, and finally, as will be shown, of freedom in general and the Four Freedoms in particular. These interpretations render impossible the true expression and enjoyment of freedom, because they deny and exclude the following truths.

1) Everything in the world is not subject to change. For example, man's divine creation, his natural condition in consequence of original sin, his last end, eternal happiness with his Creator, the immutable principles and sanctions of the moral law, man's basic physical, intellectual, moral, and spiritual wants, these *never* change.

2) Man was divinely created, and differs in kind as well as in degree from the lower animals because he possesses an intellect able to attain truth, and a will

free to choose the good. Man, moreover, is responsible for his conduct, and has to earn complete happiness by saving his immortal soul.

3) Experience is not the only source of knowledge; man also learns through instruction, and by faith in the truths of divine revelation which cannot be known fully by experience and reason. Likewise, man learns not only through his own personal experience but also by vicarious experience; that is, the experiences furnished him by others. Knowledge is the product of man's intellect; it is acquired through the characteristic operation of the intellect's powers as shown in the formation of concepts, judgments, reasoning.

4) Man does not create his own truth, or the norms governing freedom, through experience alone. There is one objective body of truth to which man must submit. This body comprises the combined wisdom of revelation and human reason. It embraces the moral law which is immutable and made known to man by conscience. To this law all conduct and the exercise of freedom must be conformed if the individual is to live fruitfully, worthily, and fulfill the obvious purpose of his creation.

5) Morality does not have its ultimate source in experience or its sanctions in the will of society. The individual's worth and dignity rest on the fact that he has a moral nature. An act is morally good when it comports with man's rational nature, and when sound reason indicates that it contributes to the attainment of his eternal destiny. Man approaches this end when he strives to achieve the proper objects of his rational powers. When any one of these powers is used contrary to its natural purpose, that action is intrinsically bad.

The ultimate sanction for morality, in addition to the truths of divine revelation governing man's last end, is: "Act against your rational nature, and you will fail of your final perfection and happiness."

6) Intelligence is one manifestation of man's spiritual soul, and through its operation knowledge is acquired, truth and certitude obtained.

7) Freedom is man's inalienable right conferred on him by his Creator. Its exercise is subject to the common good, to lawfully constituted authority, and is governed by the moral law, not by constantly "reconstructed experiences."

8) Democracy is a way of life founded and constructed on man's inalienable rights, "life, liberty, and the pursuit of happiness," which are gifts from the Creator to whom all men have obligations. It recognizes the intrinsic worth of the individual, and the moral law as governing all human conduct.

The experimentalist concept of freedom is that man, because he has the capacity for growth, acquires freedom for himself through his own experiences. Man, then, is held to be a creature of his own experiences, who exists in a free social order subject only to the authority and sanctions of his own impulses and the will of the group. He follows the bents of his own nature, reconstructs his own experiences, and literally creates his own freedom according as he satisfies "felt needs."

Now, it is patent that the satisfaction of "felt needs," unless governed and controlled by reason and the moral law, inevitably leads to individual ruin and renders impossible the proper exercise and enjoyment of freedom both by the individual and the group. Obviously, there must be an objective means, namely, authority and tradition, to limit the satisfaction of "felt needs," otherwise conflicts arise which destroy the freedom of all, and lead to the moral collapse of society.

Leonard and Eurich voice the opposition of the experimentalist to authority and tradition, together with their effects upon freedom, in the following passage:

"Experience is an effective teacher," has often been said. If one lives in a state of subservience and of strict obedience, he is likely to develop a feeling of inferiority in his ability to change the social forces of life. Men long in chains grow to love the security their chains provide. Men with a prolonged experience of contemplation grow to fear their ability to deal with the active phase of human experience; they grow to consider it secondary or even to deride it. Youth taught to accept authority, without having followed a process of arriving at a conclusion of their own, are likely to grow to be more comfortable under authority than under freedom to choose their own paths of living. They are not likely to become explorers, nor are they apt to like to live dangerously. They may choose the guidance of tradition, of authoritarian conclusions, and of complacency so long that they grow to deride change. They flee from revolution or even obvious evolution and cling to the institutions that change little or not at all. They thus lose their freedom, becoming slaves of existing conditions and cowards of the future, for free men are revolutionary men in thought and dynamic men in action.[10].

It is clear, then, that self-expression, denial of the sanctions of absolute authority, constitute the experimentalist view of freedom. This false philosophy of life

---

[10] Leonard, J. P., and Eurich, A. C. (editors), *An Evaluation of Modern Education* (New York: D. Appleton-Century Co., 1942), pp. 17–18.

encourages selfishness, lawlessness, and disparages discipline, self-sacrifice, and Christian charity.

Freedom, perforce, must be founded on a correct interpretation of man as a moral being, who is endowed with inalienable rights by his Creator, and who has a supernatural end. The concept of true freedom must embrace the correct understanding of society and its function, which is to foster and protect the material and spiritual welfare of its members. It must include, moreover, the acceptance of objective truth, and be conformed to the eternal norms which govern all reality. Since experimentalism rejects each of the foregoing necessary truths, and since it places freedom solely on a pragmatic foundation, it presents a false and exclusive interpretation of freedom.

Under experimentalism, freedom of speech and expression implies that man may say and do whatever he pleases, provided he conforms to accepted group practices and standards, and thus avoids social disapproval. Because group practices are constantly changing, and a universal moral law governing man's conduct is denied, it is obvious that such freedom is merely sheer license. By the specious argument that knowledge is attainable only by experience, and that supernatural truths and sanctions are mere figments of the imagination, designed to paralyze man's creative activity and to destroy his freedom, experimentalism dehumanizes man and perverts his very nature.

Freedom of worship is unrecognized by experimentalism, because God, the soul, the moral law are not only excluded from that philosophy, but are held to be nonexistent. Instead of being encouraged to follow the dictates of his conscience, to worship his Creator to whom he is responsible for his conduct, man is directed, rather, to worship solely the authority of the group and to conform his conduct to group purposes. He may or may not, according to his fancy, entertain belief in some kind of God, provided such belief does not interfere with his obligations to society, or cause him to act in opposition to experimentalist theories and practices. Thus, God may be interpreted on a purely natural, social, or scientific basis, and religion may be founded wholly on "religious experience." Properly defined, freedom to worship God means the ability and the duty of man to worship God as He *ought* to be worshiped by a rational being. Experimentalism, however, by denying fundamental truths and by seeking to give religion solely a scientific foundation, excludes the only basis on which the correct meaning and exercise of this freedom can be founded.

Freedom from want, according to experimentalism, means complete acceptance by man of the recognized "tested thought products" of science and experience, so that these may serve to guide all individual conduct and group activity, and thereby provide the maximum satisfaction of "felt needs." Freedom from want, then, implies the satisfaction of natural impulses and material needs. Since experimentalism denies the moral law, the principles of which must govern the fulfillment of all wants, and since it likewise excludes man's spiritual yearnings, it cannot provide, therefore, the true basis for the exercise of this freedom.

Freedom from fear is interpreted to mean absence of group disapproval, or protection of the individual from the consequences resulting from the application of social sanctions when necessary adjustments are not made rapidly and effectively. This freedom can be properly understood and expressed only when fear itself is understood in its true meaning, and not limited merely to physical, economic, and social aspects. Freedom from fear may be had in full measure when man acquires material security in his person and possessions under a well-regulated social order, and moral and spiritual security by living the good life according to God's law. But it is clear at once that experimentalism, by its very exclusivism, can provide neither the requisite social conditions nor the necessary truths on which that freedom must rest.

Obviously, then, experimentalism is a false, exclusive, materialistic philosophy of life. It presents not only an erroneous but an exclusive interpretation of the Four Freedoms by assigning to them merely a social or a scientific foundation. True freedom has a moral basis, and harmonizes with man's rational nature. Because experimentalism denies the moral foundation of freedom and wholly misinterprets man's rational nature, it cannot provide the bases of the Four Freedoms. Hence, the answer to the question, "Are the bases of the Four Freedoms found in the philosophy of experimentalism?" must be no!

TRUE PHILOSOPHY. It should be evident from the foregoing pages of this chapter that the bases of the Four Freedoms are not to be found within the fields of science, sociology, or economics; nor are they to be discovered in the false philosophies in which so many people seek them. It follows, then, that an honest inquiry into true philosophy and divine revelation might bring to light the real sources of those freedoms.

In true philosophy are found valid explanations of

man, his origin, nature, and destiny; the functions of the State, the nation, and the various forms of civil society; the meaning and the scope of freedom and the Four Freedoms; the necessity of authority; in fine, the correct principles which govern the democratic way of life, and the proper enjoyment of the values inherent therein. The plenitude and certainty of these principles and values, however, are known and realized only when religion is joined to philosophy; for religion enlightens philosophy, crowns its truths with certitude, constitutes the very cornerstone of the democratic way of life, and furnishes the ultimate sanction of all freedom. In order to comprehend fully, then, the right ordering of human life, which is quite necessary for the maximum enjoyment of freedom itself and the Four Freedoms, the guiding light of true philosophy and divinely revealed religion is an imperative need. Philosophy provides the logical foundations for freedom and valid norms which govern its use. Revealed religion, in its turn, gives certitude to those foundations, and proclaims that the norms which regulate freedom are eternal and unchangeable. Philosophy and revealed religion together set forth, moreover, the fundamental principles and the correct way by which freedom and the Four Freedoms can be implemented through education.

It is necessary, first of all, to inquire into the nature of philosophy and to discover what truths it offers as the bases of the Four Freedoms.

NATURE OF PHILOSOPHY. Philosophy is usually defined as that science which seeks to know the final causes of all things through the light of natural reason, unaided by divine revelation. It is defined, again, as love of wisdom, search for truth, or intimate knowledge of the reasons for things. Redden and Ryan give the following descriptive definition:

Philosophy is concerned with the ultimate meaning of all reality, and may be defined as the *methodical investigation of the whole of reality through its ultimate causes* in so far as those causes can be known through natural reason unaided by divine revelation. There is a force in man's nature urging him on toward truth and happiness, which is satisfied only when truth is recognized in its basic form, and when happiness becomes a reality. The science that recognizes and explains this urge for ultimate truth and happiness is philosophy, that science which treats of things according to their highest and ultimate causes.[11]

The especial province of philosophy may be more sharply defined by a brief consideration of the particular province of certain other fields of knowledge. The science of botany, for example, concerns, among other things, the study of the flower — any flower. Botany asks: To what family does the flower belong? What kind of pistil, stamen, petal, or root does it have? Biology, on the other hand, asks: How does the flower grow? What kind of cells are found in this flower? How do the cells multiply? Philosophy, however, asks: *Why* does the flower grow at all? What is its purpose in the scheme of things? What is life? Do living things differ essentially from nonliving things? Again, one of the problems which the science of sociology considers is the effects of environment on moral character. Philosophy, however, inquires whether or not there is such a thing as morality, and asks: Whence does morality

---

[11] Redden, J. D., and Ryan, F. A., *A Catholic Philosophy of Education* (Milwaukee: The Bruce Publishing Co., 1942), p. 14.

have its source? Is man responsible for his conduct? If so, to whom is he responsible, and why?

It will be seen, then, that philosophy differs from the other sciences in this, namely, that it pushes its questions and the answers to those questions farther and farther back until it comes, finally, to ultimate causes: to the last *what*, to the last *how*, to the last *why*, and to the last *Who*. Philosophy embraces all reality, and attempts to discover its ultimate reasons.

Science is concerned with facts as facts, their observation, recording, organization, generalization, and evaluation. Facts are its province. It is not concerned with the *ultimate* causes of those facts, nor with determining what those facts *ought* to be. Science takes facts as it finds them, and interprets them according to what they *are*, namely, facts. Philosophy, unlike science, is concerned not only with the *ultimate* what, why, whence, and Who, but also and especially with the ultimate *ought: what is and what ought to be.*

The knowledge or wisdom which philosophy provides is twofold: (1) knowledge of reality; and (2) knowledge of right living according to man's rational nature, final destiny, and God's eternal law. This wisdom comes to man from three sources:

1. Truths which man's intellect finds already created and known. These are accepted for study, and comprise, for example, the properties of nature, the things of nature, being and its relationships.

2. Truths which man's intellect derives by means of its power to think, reason, and judge.

3. Truths which human reason produces and which in turn enlighten the will to choose the good so that

the will consents to conduct that conforms to the commands of the moral law.

It should be clear, of course, that there is but one true philosophy, because there is only one source of all truth, namely, God, who, being truth itself, cannot contradict Himself. The Creator has manifested His eternal wisdom to man in a twofold manner: (1) by the works of creation which man can know through reason; (2) by divine revelation, especially through Jesus Christ, who in His own words states: "I am the way and the truth and the life" (John 14:6). A partial knowledge of the truths of revelation is attainable by human reason; but a more extensive and intimate knowledge is gained by faith in the authority of God's truth. Complete knowledge and understanding of these revealed truths, however, can be had only when the individual possesses, in eternal life, the beatific vision.

These two manifestations of divine wisdom are organized, systematized, and studied as two separate branches of philosophy: (1) natural philosophy; and (2) supernatural philosophy or theology. The distinction between these two branches is found in their sources, in the content of the manifestation, and the manner in which it is studied and applied. Natural philosophy studies phenomena in the natural order, such as man, nature, things, causes, relations; and certain truths in the supernatural order, such as the existence of God, the immortality of the soul, the freedom of the will, the norms of right conduct, solely in and through the light of man's *natural reason*. Supernatural philosophy studies divinely revealed truths in the light of *faith* and *dogma*. It does not depend on natural reason alone, but attains certainty solely on the authority of God. It accepts the truths of revelation, systematizes them, and applies them in regulating conduct.

There are certain fundamental truths which have been made known to man by divine revelation because they are beyond his power to know with certainty by the light of his own unaided reason. These truths are essential to the right ordering of man's life, the exercise of the Four Freedoms, and the work of education by means of which these freedoms are implemented. These truths concern man's origin, his nature as a consequence of original sin, his redemption by Jesus Christ, and his final destiny.

In the broad meaning of the term, true philosophy includes both branches, namely, natural philosophy and supernatural philosophy. In its restricted meaning, philosophy embraces that knowledge which is gained solely by the use of natural reason. In this book, the broad meaning of the term philosophy is implied and used.

It may be said, in fine, that philosophy supplies the speculative and practical knowledge which interprets correctly man, his nature, his last end, the purpose and function of society, the democratic way of life, the meaning, scope, and limitations of freedom, in brief, all reality. It is patent, then, that the true interpretation and correct exercise of freedom must have this knowledge as their bases.

As stated earlier, philosophy is concerned with the explanation of the ultimate causes of all things. Now, a philosophy of life embraces those speculative and practical truths which have a bearing, more or less direct, on man's life and behavior. It is a purposeful attempt to apply in every aspect of man's individual and social life the teachings of the particular philosophy to which one assents. It goes without saying that this ought to mean for each individual the teachings of true philosophy. A philosophy of life implies, moreover, the view that a person takes of himself, the world, and his fellow men. This view is based on the fundamental truths which one holds or accepts. Sometimes this "view" is known as the individual's "world view." It embraces his own decisions and convictions as to what life is all about. Such convictions rest upon those fundamental, ultimate truths which the individual consciously or unconsciously accepts for himself as true and final. Thus, one's philosophy of life is based, primarily, on the truths one accepts as valid and guiding. It is of primary importance, of course, that these truths by which one guides one's conduct should be absolutely true in themselves, since they establish norms which govern all conduct and, hence, must govern also the exercise and enjoyment of the Four Freedoms and their implementation. Only by the acceptance and the application of these truths, supplied by philosophy, can man live abundantly; exercise his inalienable rights; enjoy the blessings of freedom to the maximum degree; be educated according to his rational nature; fulfill his purposes in the world; and finally attain eternal happiness with his Creator.

REVELATION. In simple terms, revelation may be defined as the direct manifestation to man by God of His will and His laws governing all reality. It is the means by which God directly passes on to man those truths which ordinarily transcend man's natural power or inclination to know and live by. Many of these, such as the mysteries of faith, would remain unknown unless directly communicated to man. It is this communication of the divine deposit of truths that constitutes what is called *divine revelation*.

It should be made clear that even though man can attain through reason a distant glimmer of some of these truths, nevertheless, full certainty can be had only from the fact that they have been divinely revealed. Man cannot acquire the infinite knowledge of these truths and mysteries until he attains the beatific vision in the hereafter. Again, revelation is a supernatural means used by God to affirm certain truths, the discovery of which *per se* lies within the power of human reason. The essence of revelation lies in the fact that it is the direct word of God transmitted to man and available for his acceptance. It comprises a body of content expressing the divine Will, and, as such, cannot be subjected to the test of experience or to private interpretation.

The decree *"Lamentabili,"*[11a] July 3, 1907, positively declares that the dogmas which the Church holds to be divinely revealed are "truths which have come down to us from heaven." In condemnation of a contradictory proposition, the decree avers that revelation is not "an interpretation of religious facts which the human mind has acquired by its own strenuous efforts." Rather, revelation supplies positive truths governing man, his nature, and final destiny which constitute that "deposit of faith" given in its entirety by Jesus Christ

---

[11a] Denziger, H., et Baunwart, C. (Ed. J. B. Umberg, S.J.), *Enchiridion Symbolorum,* Editio 21–23 (Friburgi Brisgovial: Herder and Co., 1937), pp. 564–569, Nos. 2001–2065a.

to His Apostles. The Church accepts this deposit, and to it nothing can be added or taken away. When the question arises of interpreting or defining doctrine, the sole point is whether the truth is found in scripture or in apostolic tradition.

The question may be asked whether or not revelation is necessary for man, his freedom, and the manner of living essential to the attainment of his purposes in this world and of his ultimate happiness in the hereafter. It may be answered at once with certainty that revelation crowns, without any possibility of error, all man's legitimate purposes and gives full sanction to the proper expression of his freedom and his inalienable rights. Revelation is necessary because God destined man for beatitude. This destiny transcends man's natural powers and the ends of society. The fact of this beatitude (man's supernatural end and the means to attain it) must be known by man with full certainty. Revelation, moreover, is morally necessary for man to obtain through the use of his God-given powers that further knowledge of the natural law which is essential for the right ordering of his life. It is true that, under certain exceptional conditions, individuals may have attained, entirely through their own rational efforts, that knowledge of the natural law and have lived according to its teachings in a manner sufficient to achieve beatitude. The Church teaches, however, that this is the case for only a few persons; that for the mass of mankind revelation is necessary. Revelation gives security and certainty, because it separates truth from error, so that man, unable or unwilling to discover and live by the full knowledge of the moral law through his own efforts alone, can pursue with certitude, on the infallible foundations of faith, his material purposes and spiritual destiny.

What, then, constitutes the content of revelation? Revelation makes known to man the following: (1) truths of the natural law; (2) mysteries of faith and religion; and (3) positive laws concerning divine worship. Revelation, furthermore, crowns with certitude the truths of philosophy which supply the only valid bases of the Four Freedoms.

BASIC TRUTHS AND FREEDOM. In order to discover and understand the valid bases of the Four Freedoms, it is essential to set forth, first of all, the fundamental truths which govern those freedoms. They are as follows:

1. The universe was created by God who in His providence conserves and rules it.

2. Man was created by God to know, love, and serve Him here on earth, and thus attain eternal happiness with Him hereafter.

3. Man is composed of body and soul, joined in substantial union. Thus, man is not body alone nor soul alone, but body and soul united to form one substance.

4. There exists in God an eternal law obliging all men to do what is good and to avoid what is evil. This law derives from the archetypal ideas existing in the divine essence. Applied to all nature, it is commonly called "the natural law," for it obliges all created beings to act according to their essential nature. Applied to human conduct, this law is usually known as "the moral law."

5. Since man is obliged by the natural law to act

according to his rational nature, he possesses a conscience which urges him to do good and to avoid evil. Conscience is not a separate "faculty" in man. It is the judgment one makes of the rightness or wrongness of a human act. A "human act" is an act that one is free to do or not to do.

6. Man is endowed by his Creator with an intellect by which he can know truth, and a free will by which he can embrace and follow it.

7. Man is responsible for his conduct in regard to his God, his neighbor, and himself. He must conform his conduct to the eternal norms of the moral law. The moral law exists outside of man. It is obligatory on every man. It is unchanging in itself, and, hence, is not affected in any way by social changes.

8. God gave man the power to learn certain truths in the natural order; and God has revealed to man certain truths in the supernatural order, which truths, unless divinely revealed, would be unknown to man.

9. There are certain supernatural aids to conduct which transcend man's natural powers, for example, prayer, grace, and the sacraments.

10. Because of original sin, man's intellect is less able than in the preternatural state to attain truth, his will is less able to seek the good, and his nature is more inclined to evil.

11. Man's fallen nature, due to original sin, was redeemed by Jesus Christ. Through baptism, certain supernatural gifts are restored to man, but certain effects of original sin remain.

12. Man, by his very nature, is a social being, and, as such, has duties toward society and is influenced by society.

13. The worth of the individual human being is founded on the following truths: his creation to the image and likeness of God; his immortal soul; his rational and moral nature; his freedom of the will; his inalienable rights; his redemption by Jesus Christ; his membership in the mystical body of Christ.

14. Man is endowed by his Creator with certain inalienable rights, namely, life, liberty, and the pursuit of happiness. For the proper understanding of these rights, man has an intellect, and for their proper exercise, a free will. The formal object of man's intellect is *truth;* and the formal object of his free will is *the good.* Thus, man is said to possess all the powers necessary for him to do good and avoid evil, and thereby attain his immediate purposes in this world and his ultimate end with God in heaven.

It should be noted that the foregoing truths, derived from philosophy in the broad meaning of that term, fall within the following categories: philosophical, philosophical-theological, and theological. The term *philosophical* applies to those truths which can readily be known to human reason. *Philosophical-theological* refers to truths of which some far, faint glimmer can be caught by human reason, but which, for completeness and certitude, require the full light of divine revelation. The word *theological* is used to describe truths which reason, of itself, could not know and, hence, are divinely revealed. These truths, then, coming from both philosophy and divine revelation, supply the only valid bases of the Four Freedoms.

In summarizing, now, this discussion of the valid bases of the Four Freedoms, it should be said that these bases are not found in the fields of science, sociology, economics; nor are they provided by the false materialistic philosophies of naturalism, socialism, exaggerated nationalism, communism, or experimentalism. Valid bases are found only in the truths of philosophy and divine revelation.

Freedom, as stated on earlier pages, is an inalienable right of man bestowed on him as a gift by his Creator, and in its exercise must conform to the sanctions of legitimate authority and the moral law. Freedom, then, has a moral foundation and depends for its existence on divine origin and authority. Such dependence offers the strongest guarantee of conduct directed to the promotion of the common good materially, and the ultimate good of the individual spiritually. In order to interpret infallibly the ultimate good, both material and spiritual, true philosophy and revelation are needed. Therein are set forth the only complete and valid concepts explaining man, his origin, nature, and destiny; the functions of the State, the nation, and the various forms of civil society; the nature, meaning, scope, and limitations of freedom and liberty; in fine, the fundamental truths which govern the democratic way of life and the enjoyment of the values inherent therein.

The democratic way of life, which flows from the teachings of Christian philosophy, includes certain fundamental truths upon which it depends both for its existence and preservation. Unless these, and the values that flow from them, are known, respected, and upheld, the democratic way of life runs the grave peril of utter destruction. Thus, philosophy supplies this knowledge and these values, and revelation crowns them with certitude. These truths set forth the binding obligation of the moral law; they demonstrate and uphold the worth and dignity of the individual; they point the way infallibly to the attainment of man's material purposes and supernatural end. The full richness of the values set forth by philosophy is realized only in religion, which, in fact, constitutes the very cornerstone of the democratic way of life and supplies the ultimate sanctions of all freedom. This is evident from the fact that religion asserts the existence of God, the immortality of the soul, the freedom of the will, faith in divine providence, and God's law as binding on all men in conscience and in conduct. These truths and their acceptance must be made an integral part of education, if education is to have any real meaning and purpose. Likewise, they must permeate all individual and social conduct, if the democratic way of life is finally to prevail. When education is thus made meaningful and social living thus made purposeful, then it may be said that the individual becomes fitted and disposed to exercise and enjoy, to the full measure, the values conferred on him by the Four Freedoms.

The guiding light of true philosophy and divine revelation provides the only intelligent and effective means, for the right ordering of life needed to enjoy the maximum of freedom itself and the Four Freedoms, correctly defined and delimited. Taken together, philosophy and divine revelation supply the valid bases of the Four Freedoms.

Chapter III

THE FOUR FREEDOMS AND DEMOCRACY

INTRODUCTION. In order that the Four Freedoms may become a reality, and flourish in their full meaning, it is necessary that the way of life under which man lives should be the *right way of life,* constructed on the fundamental truths supplied by philosophy and revelation. Only when these truths are applied in all individual, social, and civic conduct can freedom be had, and the Four Freedoms exercised and enjoyed to the maximum degree. This right way of life is the Christian way of life. There can be no democratic way of life, or "American way of life," that is not essentially the Christian way of life.

It is the purpose of this chapter to interpret democracy and its underlying principles. It will be demonstrated that the Four Freedoms, in their full meaning and correct expression, can flourish only under a right interpretation of democracy itself, which will be seen to be one and the same with the way of life taught and exemplified by Jesus Christ.

MEANING OF DEMOCRACY. Democracy has its origins in human nature itself, correctly understood. It is constructed on the fact that man is by his very nature a social being. Its actualization is directed by and dependent on this social fact, as well as on the fact that man is by nature free to choose the good among motives. Democracy is really a uniform manner of living based on a universal moral law, the immutable law of God. This law presents the unchanging principles of morality which embrace Christian charity and justice, and interpret the divinely instituted plan according to which man must conform his conduct in order to attain eternal salvation. This law, moreover, upholds and governs man's inalienable rights and their expression, and gives valid sanctions to the democratic way of life. When man acknowledges that his inalienable rights are gifts from his Creator, to whom he owes duties, his will is more likely to be disposed to conform to God's law. Such disposition is the very basis of all freedom and democracy. When this truth is recognized and applied, namely, that man must know God better and conform his individual and social conduct to God's divine will, then it may be rightly said that man is ready for purposeful democratic living and for the full exercise of the Four Freedoms.

In the broad meaning of the term, then, democracy is the Christian way of life. It is founded on man's true origin, his nature and final destiny, the nature and purposes of society, the mutual relationship between man and society as governed by the correct interpretation of freedom and authority made known by Jesus Christ. Concerning man's nature, democracy recognizes the dignity and worth of the individual as transcending all material purposes and ends, and it emphasizes the fundamental truth that society exists for man, not man for society. Democracy, moreover, acknowledges God as the Creator of man and the State, and as the source of all rights, duties, authority, and freedom. Thus Monsignor Kerby writes:

Democracy is primarily social, moral, and spiritual and secondarily political. It is a philosophy of life as well as a theory of government. It is inspired by a noble concept of the individual, of the dignity of his person, the sanctity of his rights, the claim of his powers to normal development. Democratic institutions taken in conjunction with sturdy home life, strong community sense, reasonable self-control, true valuations, healthy respect for religion and obedience to its spiritual teaching and general education can scarcely fail of their high inspiring promise to humanity.[1]

In a restricted sense, that is, politically considered, democracy is only one form of government which natural civil society takes. Thus, a democracy may exist under various forms or names and with varying degrees of organization. Each of these forms of government, if it constitutes a democracy in the full meaning of the term must be ruled by, must accept, and practice in its manner of operation and living, eternal moral principles. Failure of any form of government to accept the sanctions of moral and religious teachings results in distortion and frustration of human nature and its divinely instituted purposes. Such failure means, basically, that the moral law, requiring all men to conform their conduct to its tenets, is disregarded, and that its sanctions are ignored. Under these conditions, it is impossible for man's inalienable rights and the Four Freedoms to receive recognition and expression. Hutchins emphasizes the moral basis of democracy in the following passage:

---

[1] Kerby, W. J., *The Social Mission of Charity* (New York: The Macmillan Co., 1930), p. 25.

Since the freedom of autonomy is the end of human life, everything else in life should be a means to it and should be subordinate to it as means must be to ends. This is true of material goods, which are means, and a very necessary one, but not an end. It is true of the state, which is an indispensable means, but not an end. It is true of all human activities and all human desires: they are all ordered to, and must be judged by, the end of moral and intellectual development.

The political organization must be tested by its conformity to these ideals. Its basis is moral. Its end is the good for man. Only democracy has this basis. Only democracy has this end. If we do not believe in this basis or this end, we do not believe in democracy. These are the principles which we must defend if we are to defend democracy.[2]

When each person understands that his inalienable rights come from God as free gifts, and accepts the duties that flow from these rights, then it may be said that he is fitted and disposed to participate in the enjoyment of those freedoms inherent in true democratic life. Such acceptance is basic in the Christian way of life, the democratic ideal, and serves to enhance all the civic and social virtues which characterize "the good citizen."

Kerwin describes the essential features of democracy in the following passage:

It is the sole form of government today where the sanctity of the individual, the responsibility of the individual, and the freedom of the individual are recognized and respected. Men under the democratic form may be free to become great sinners, but they are also free to become great saints. Men are free to abuse the liberty given them as men abuse the free will that God has given them, but

---

[2] Hutchins, R. M., *Education for Freedom* (Baton Rouge, La.: Louisiana University Press, 1943), pp. 92–93.

without that freedom men do not attain to that fully developed temporal or spiritual maturity — responsible citizens of the State, and responsible sons of the Church. Only in the democratic States today is the thoroughly Catholic doctrine of natural rights recognized in theory and in practice. Only in the democratic States does man still possess a sphere of action free of governmental control and interference. Surely in this, our day, Catholic preference for democracy should be widely known — for that democracy where our churches and schools flourish, where our people freely attend the divine services, where our priests are free to teach the Gospel, where our press suffers no oppression from governmental censors, where our voices are heard in the councils of the nation, and where our youths may be reared in the fear and love of God without bowing down in idolatry before a mere man who calls himself leader and who thinks of himself as God.[3]

PRINCIPLES OF DEMOCRACY. It has been emphasized that democracy is a way of life, essentially the Christian way of life, constructed on the infallible truths of right philosophy and divine revelation. A brief discussion of these fundamental truths, which constitute the principles upon which democracy is based, will show their importance and their applicability to that way of life in which, alone, the Four Freedoms can be exercised and enjoyed.

1. True democracy acknowledges that the dignity and worth of the individual are based on the following facts: his divine creation; his essentially moral nature; his inalienable rights; his redemption by Jesus Christ; and his membership in the mystical body of Christ.

True democracy recognizes that man has a dual

---

[3] "Public Concerns of an American Catholic," *Social Problems* (Philadelphia: Sociology Department of the College of Chestnut Hill), Vol. I, No. 7, Sept., 1938, p. 74.

nature, physical and spiritual, body and soul joined in substantial union; and that his destiny, being supernatural and, hence, beyond the limits of this material universe, transcends all group purposes and social institutions. Thus, democracy and democratic society are founded on man's divine origin and destiny. On these latter rests his dignity; and from them come his rights and his freedom. Pointing out this basic truth, President Roosevelt, in his message to Congress on the state of the Union, January 4, 1939, made the following statement:

Storms from abroad directly challenge three institutions indispensable to Americans, now as always. The first is religion. It is the source of the other two — democracy and international good faith. Religion, by teaching man his relationship to God, gives the individual a sense of his own dignity and teaches him to respect himself by respecting his neighbors.[4]

As stated above, man's destiny serves to demonstrate his worth because it implies an end which exists beyond the limits of society or any institution in the material order. The attainment of this end requires the knowledge and practice of religion. Religion is not man made. It cannot be founded on a materialistic, naturalistic, scientific, humanistic, or socialistic basis. Religion, to be true, must be divine in its origin, its content, and its sanctions. Only that religion revealed by Jesus Christ, which teaches and continually emphasizes in its every aspect the worth of the *individual,* can properly, and with certitude, give

---

[4] Roosevelt, F. D., "Address to the Congress of the United States on the State of the Union," January 4, 1939; *Vital Speeches,* Vol. 5, January 15, 1939, p. 211.

dignity to human personality, or stability and permanence to democracy.

Father James T. Cronin, emphasizing the *primacy* of the individual in the democratic way of life, writes as follows:

When we look for the most fundamental premise of . . . democracy, we find that it consists of a concept or appreciation of human nature that is at the same time most illusive, most fragile, and yet most real. The democratic premise that the individual is unique, possessing an inherent worth not given him by society, is as fragile as any ideal is fragile and yet it has a reality far more substantial than this paper.

Ultimately the democratic concept of life and living must perish from the earth if a sufficient body of men do not hold fast to the basic premise of the unique and inviolable individual. Democracy does not rest on freedom from restraint. It does not depend on universal suffrage. It probably can persist without freedom of speech or press. Physical liberty, suffrage, freedom for the spoken and written word — these are external expressions and safeguards of a deeply fundamental truth of human nature.

Democracy concedes, of course, certain rights of the group over the individual; it grants that in certain restricted areas the good of the individual is to be placed in a position subordinate to the welfare of society. Nevertheless, democracy recognizes that it must wither and die as a distinctive way of life if it abandons the primacy of the individual.[5]

2. Democracy holds that civil society exists for man and not man for society: both have duties to each other. Man is a member of society and, hence, cannot exist independent of his fellow men. He has a supernatural destiny and a dignity above the rest of creation,

_____

[5] Cronin, J. T., *The Individual Versus Society* (Private Printing: Fordham University, Department of Education, 1937).

and must achieve this destiny through his own efforts and conduct in a material world. In thus striving to attain his proper end, the satisfaction of his material and spiritual needs is enhanced or hindered, as the case may be, by his social interactions with his fellow men. In order to obtain that sufficiency of material goods required for the practice of virtue, man must participate in the affairs of society. In this process of participation, mutual benefits are derived both by man and by society.

Man's relationship to society is emphasized by Leo XIII in the following passage:

Man's natural instinct moves him to live in civil society. Isolated, he cannot provide himself with the necessary requirements of life, nor procure the means of developing his mental and moral faculties. It is, therefore, divinely ordained that he should lead his life — be it domestic, social, or civil — in contact with his fellow men, where alone his several wants can be adequately supplied. But no society can remain united without some one in command, directing all to strive earnestly for the common good. Hence, every civilized community must have a ruling authority, and this authority, no less than society itself, has its source in nature, and consequently has God for its author.[6]

It should be remembered that society exists to serve man's needs, and thereby contribute in the maximum to his material and spiritual development. Man does not exist for society, or the state, or the nation, or the proletariat, as false philosophies contend. God is the efficient cause of society, and the welfare of man is its final end. This fact gives significance and validity to the

---

[6] Leo XIII, *Immortale Dei, Social Wellsprings* (Milwaukee: The Bruce Publishing Co., 1940), Vol. I, p. 66.

meaning and function of the democratic way of life.

Man is, then, in certain aspects, independent of society; in others, he is dependent on society, and must subordinate himself to its legitimate purposes. He is independent of society because he has within himself an immortal soul destined for an end which transcends all social purposes and ideals, and hence cannot be subjected to or controlled by merely social forces or causes. This supernatural independence of man requires that he possess certain inalienable rights to life, liberty, and the pursuit of happiness, which cannot be usurped by any power on earth, because the exercise of these rights is essential to the attainment of his supernatural destiny. Democracy has the unique duty, therefore, of facilitating the pursuit of the individual's destiny by fostering the correct expression of these rights, and by encouraging the discharge of the duties implied thereby.

On the other hand, because man possesses a social nature he is dependent on society for his material well-being, and subject, therefore, to its legitimate authority. In consequence, man has social duties which he must discharge, one of which is his definite obligation to contribute to the common good of his fellow men. The fulfillment of these duties, among others, is requisite for man to attain eternal happiness with his Creator.

Democracy, then, rightly envisages society as a means to an end, namely, to foster and promote the common good of mankind. This implies that man, a person distinct in himself, with a dignity beyond the rest of creation, may pursue and attain his legitimate ends aided by all the means at the disposal of democratic society. Man, a social and political animal, truly depends for his life, sustenance, and personal development on that security and fostering care supplied by society.

3. Democracy teaches that freedom is an endowment of man from his Creator, enabling him to fulfill his purposes and to seek his final end. Likewise, democracy holds that authority is a necessary means given to man by his Creator to guide him in the proper use of his freedom. Since man must live in society, and society has the obligation to promote the common good, order is necessary. This order must assume a form that implies on the part of society authority sufficient to fulfill its assigned obligations to its members, namely, the promotion of the common good. Both authority and freedom are means, never ends. The former gives order and unity to the social group in promoting the common good, which is the advancement of the material and spiritual well-being of every person. The latter is always directed to man's ultimate good. Authority, then, rightly interpreted and applied, aids man in the proper exercise of his freedom.

It may be said, therefore, that man is truly free in his own acts when he submits to the rule of properly constituted authority; and this is precisely what democracy teaches and expects of all its members. When the individual abides by the moral law in his every form of conduct, he has acquired that measure of self-control which may be described as *moral democracy* in his own interior life. Law can never be explained in its true meaning as placing restrictions on the exercise of man's freedom; rather, it is the protector of freedom and liberty. Thus, under democracy, freedom and authority are complementary.

4. Democracy asserts that all rights and duties have

their source in God, and must be directed in their exercise to the fulfillment of the individual and social purposes for which they exist. It is evident, then, that democracy accepts the interpretation of true philosophy which holds that rights and duties are founded on man's God-given nature and end, as well as on the nature and end of the state. Now, man has a supernatural destiny, and in order to attain this he has been endowed with inalienable or natural rights. These rights imply and require the acceptance of duties. Ryan and Millar describe these natural rights as follows:

Life and liberty cover a very large part of the field of natural rights; the pursuit of happiness implies the rights of marriage and property, which embrace the remainder of that field. Man's natural rights may, therefore, be summarized as those of life, liberty, marriage, and property. Liberty is, of course, a wide conception extending to physical movement, education, religion, speech, and writing. Under the head of life is included immunity from all forms of arbitrary physical assault. All these rights belong to the citizen as a human being because they are all necessary for his existence, for the development of his personality, for reasonable human living, and for the attainment of the end which God commands him to attain. In the United States they are all likewise rights of the citizen as a citizen.[7]

5. Democracy holds that all men are equal in origin, nature, and purpose, but not in interests, talents, and abilities; that the majority should rule provided such rule does no violence to the individual, his inalienable rights, or to the moral law governing all individual and social conduct. It will be seen then, by this prin-

---

[7] Ryan, J., and Millar, M., *The State and the Church* (New York: The Macmillan Co., 1937), p. 277.

ciple, that democracy envisages the correct meaning and scope of the concepts "equality" and "majority rule."

All men are equal in origin and ultimate end. They are equal in the dignity and worth of human personality and before the law. Each human soul is equally precious in the eyes of the heavenly Father. Individuals, however, differ in talents, abilities, and vocational aptitudes, according to the disposition of divine providence. For the common good, it is essential that society recognize and utilize individual differences, as well as classify and develop talents according to their essential contribution to the well-being of society. Some are best fitted to lead; others have creative, productive talents; others, again, are suited to be followers, consumers as it were. All of these must be given their proper place in society. Every individual should be trained and equipped to contribute in some way to social betterment. Democracy seeks to utilize the services of everyone, no matter how small that service; and its progress and prosperity rest on the fact that everyone can have gainful and fruitful employment and earn a living in peace and security.

By the concept "majority rule," democracy implies a political means or governmental procedure wherein, by "the consent of the governed," sovereignty is transferred to the majority under the dictum "the greatest good for the greatest number." This rule by the majority, however, is not a source of authority or rights, or a transfer of these, for neither rights nor authority can be alienated; moreover, it does not necessarily imply the imposition of duties which are binding on all men in conscience. The majority group becomes merely the trustee, as it were, of the rights of the minority. As such it has the function of preserving these rights, properly understood and interpreted. Therefore, no majority ruling can, with justice, deprive any man of his rights or limit their expression except in terms of their *legitimate* exercise and enjoyment.

One cannot emphasize too frequently that rights, authority, duties have their source primarily in God, and only secondarily in the state and the family, and this by virtue of their divine institution. The authority of the state and family comes from God, and is entrusted to those who rule in accordance with the democratic principle of "divided sovereignty," by "the consent of the governed." This authority is improperly interpreted when it is asserted that the people themselves are autonomous and the source of all authority and rights, because in this contention are found the roots of despotism.

The foregoing principles of democracy, founded on the truths of philosophy and divine revelation, indicate the essentially Christian structure of the democratic way of life. They may be restated briefly as follows: (1) The dignity and worth of the individual are recognized in his divine origin, his nature, and his final end. (2) Civil society exists for man and not man for society. (3) Freedom and authority come from God, and are governed by His eternal law. (4) All rights and duties have their origin and sanction ultimately in God. (5) The concepts "equality" and "majority rule" are interpreted and limited by the moral law.

When these principles are applied strictly in conformity to the teachings of religion, democracy takes on its full meaning and truly becomes another term to describe the Christian way of life. In such a mode of life, the Four Freedoms can function, and flourish without let or hindrance. Under no other interpretation of democracy or its principles can the true expression of the Four Freedoms be effected, and that atmosphere and environment be created which will guarantee their proper implementation by education.

INTERPRETATIONS OF DEMOCRACY. It is important to distinguish between certain restricted meanings and applications of democracy, such as political, economic, and philosophical, and democracy correctly and totally conceived as one with the Christian way of life, founded and constructed on principles derived from true philosophy and divine revelation. This latter view of democracy has already been presented. A brief discussion of each of the restricted interpretations will now be set forth, together with their interrelationships to the Four Freedoms.

1. POLITICAL. This restricted interpretation of democracy is concerned primarily with the organization and functioning of a right form of government. Political democracy is constructed on the principle that the individual, by virtue of his worth, dignity, and inalienable rights, is qualified to choose the form of government that best serves his welfare. In this matter of choice it is not the individual as an isolated unit who acts, but the individual considered in the collective meaning, the sum total of the group, the community, comprising all who make up the social unit. In this meaning, the power to rule is said to belong to the community, properly understood as a composite of individuals. The goal of civil society, then, is the welfare of the community at large, the aggregate of those persons who are its members.

According to Aristotle, there are two objectives of

government, namely justice and happiness. Justice implies that no individual or group acquire enough power to dominate or wrong any other person. Happiness implies that every opportunity be afforded the individual to acquire that sufficiency of material goods required for his personal well-being, and for the practice of virtue, which is essential to the attainment of his spiritual sanctification. The quest for happiness is a natural striving of man.

Rulers must fashion and enforce laws on the basis of this universal justice in order to assist man in the attainment of his material progress as well as ultimate happiness. These laws must be governed always by the immutable norms of the moral law. Now, in the formulation of civil law, the one object continually to be kept in view is the common good. This latter must be envisaged and interpreted according to man's true origin, nature, and purposes. It must be subjected, temporarily, to the juridical consent of the governed, and, eternally, to the injunctions of the divine law. Leo XIII expressed the correct function of laws as follows:

In political affairs, and in all matters civil, the laws aim at securing the common good, and are not framed according to the delusive caprices and opinions of the mass of the people, but in accordance with truth and by justice; the ruling powers are invested with a sacredness more than human, and are withheld from deviating from the path of duty, and from overstepping the bounds of rightful authority; and the obedience of citizens is rendered with a feeling of honour and dignity, since obedience is not the servitude of man to man, but submission to the will of God, exercising His sovereignty through the medium of men. Granting this to be undeniable, we cannot but realize that the high office of rulers should be held in respect; that public authority should be constantly and faithfully obeyed; that no act of sedition should be committed; and that the civic order of the commonwealth should be maintained as sacred.[8]

Francesco Suárez, a Spanish Jesuit, in his *De Legibus* sets forth clearly the two dominant principles of democratic government: (1) the principle that the people are the source and immediate origin of political power, and may retain that power in themselves; (2) the principle of "divided sovereignty" which asserts that sovereignty rests first in the people, but with proper restrictions and conditions may be delegated to representatives or rulers under a legitimate form of government. The authority, then, which rulers and governmental officials exercise, comes directly by delegation from the people. Hence, political power is not resident in a ruler or king by divine right but in those governed.

These two principles defined and defended by Suárez, and accepted by the democratic form of government in the United States, which in reality constitutes a republic, distinguish that government from any other found in history. These principles, philosophically sound and true, were adopted by the Founding Fathers and incorporated into the Constitution of the United States. As a consequence of the acceptance of these principles, recognition is given to each of the following truths, which make possible the only conditions under which the Four Freedoms can exist and flourish: (1) Man has inalienable rights which come from his Creator. (2) Just powers are derived only from the consent of the governed. (3) The state exists for

---

[8] Leo XIII, *Immortale Dei, op. cit.,* p. 74.

man. (4) Government must protect minority rights, since all men are equal before the law. (5) The individual's freedom comes from God. (6) The exercise of all authority is governed by the moral law. (7) Man has the right and the duty to worship God.

The Founding Fathers wisely and prudently provided a system of "checks and balances" to insure the freedom of all under the democratic way of life. Evidence of this is seen in the specific powers granted to each of the three branches of government, namely, the executive, the legislative, and the judicial. The purpose of these "checks and balances" was to protect not only the primacy of the individual, and the rights of the minority, but also to deter the majority in the exercise of their constitutional powers, from any violation of true democratic principles and practices. Despite every possibility of change in political power, and the use of that power, the rights of the individual citizen are guaranteed by the Bill of Rights in the Constitution and by the proper functioning of representative government. When the inalienable rights of all citizens are recognized, upheld, and given full expression according to their proper meaning, and when democratic government is something more than mere rule by party, pressure groups, big business, or labor; then government is truly "of the people, by the people, and for the people." Then freedom can be fully exercised and enjoyed. Promotion of the democratic way of life is the function of government in a republic, such as the United States. The correct meaning of this republicanism is brought out by Hoffman in the following passage:

Unfortunately, in a world that has so largely lost its historical memory and faith in the Christian God and therefore is searching to find some substitute absolute, not much thought is given to that sane republicanism which is the common political tradition of Christendom. Most men, indeed, appear to have no notion of what a Republic actually is, fancying vaguely that it is merely a State without a king. The Christian political thinker, however, knows what it is; knows that it is the public thing maintained by a multitude of private "things"; that it is not an absolute but contingent reality; that it belongs to the community, not the community to it. Only where it is upheld, and by a community which in its turn recognizes a dependence on yet higher powers, can men discharge freely and in reasonable peace their dual duties to Caesar and to God.[9]

It should be emphasized that dangers exist, at the present time, which threaten the stability and permanence of the democratic way of life. Certain individuals or groups, taking advantage of the liberties granted and guaranteed by the Constitution of the United States, seek to substitute for democratic government a government of class or party, which usurps power and denies or ignores the intrinsic worth of the individual. George Washington warned against such dangers in the following words:

Toward the preservation of your government, and the permanency of your present happy state, it is requisite, not only that you steadily discountenance irregular oppositions to its acknowledged authority, but also that you resist with care the spirit of innovation upon its principles, however specious the pretexts. One method of assault may be to effect, in the forms of the Constitution, alterations which will impair the energy of the system, and thus to undermine what cannot be directly overthrown. . . .

But let there be no change by usurpation, for though this, in one instance, may be the instrument of good, it is

[9] Hoffman, R., *Tradition and Progress* (Milwaukee: The Bruce Publishing Co., 1938), pp. 128–129.

the customary weapon by which free governments are destroyed. The precedent must always greatly overbalance in permanent evil any partial or transient benefit which use can at any time yield.[10]

As stated previously, the proper function of democratic government is to promote the common good. Promotion of the common good implies the adoption of those means and techniques through governmental legislation and action which preserve life, uphold man's dignity, give maximum expression to his inalienable rights, and foster the correct exercise of freedom among individuals. Thus, governmental action in the interests of the common good may enact legislation required to improve standards of living, to prosecute a just war, to improve public health and sanitation, to secure freedom from want, to promote cultural and vocational education; in fine, to foster every lawful means which contributes to the material and spiritual well-being and advancement of the individual citizen.

2. ECONOMIC. It is an indisputable fact that for "life, liberty, and the pursuit of happiness," a sufficiency of material goods is essential, not only for man's temporal well-being but also for the practice of virtue.[11] Man, then, requires a modicum of economic goods in order that he may live and bring up his children in security and freedom from want. He requires food, shelter, clothing, and other primary necessities of life. In order to provide these he must have opportunity for employment in his calling and receive "a living wage." There must be, therefore, what might well be called

---

[10] Washington, G., "Farewell Address to the People of the United States, September 17, 1796," *The American Citizens Handbook* (Washington, D. C.: National Education Association, 1941), pp. 232, 235.
[11] Cf. Ch. I, pp. 27–28.

economic democracy, whose principles ought to govern the conditions under which man labors and satisfies his basic physical and social needs.

The principles on which democracy itself is founded, drawn as they are from philosophy and revelation, must promote the common good in a positive and effective manner by their direct application in the field of economics. This truth is expressed in a most cogent manner by Pius XI in the following passage:

For, though economic order and moral discipline are guided each by its own principles in its own sphere, it is false that the two orders are so distinct and alien that the former in no way depends on the latter. The so-called laws of economics, derived from the nature of earthly goods and from the qualities of human body and soul, determine what aims are unattainable or attainable in economic matters and what means are therefore necessary. On the other hand, reason itself clearly deduces from the nature of things and from the individual and social character of man what is the end and object of the whole economic order assigned by God the Creator.[12]

Democracy cannot function completely or successfully unless true "economic democracy" is effectively actualized. Those who possess economic power, therefore, must employ that power in conformity to Christian principles and ideals; otherwise, all efforts to make democracy work will eventually be unavailing. In no small measure, then, are certain freedoms dependent for their exercise and enjoyment on a *right* interpretation and actualization of economic democracy. So far, in the world at large, economic democracy has not been applied in the social order to the extent that every

---

[12] Pius XI, *Quadragesimo Anno, Social Wellsprings* (Milwaukee: The Bruce Publishing Co., 1942), Vol. II, p. 192.

individual, through his own labors and creative talents, can pursue his vocational interests and attain the sufficiency of goods necessary for freedom from want and freedom from fear.

The economic foundations of democracy rest in man's right to possess private property, something over which he can exercise his individual control. This right is rooted in man's very nature; it is not a right given by the state. Leo XIII expressed this fact as follows:

> For every man has by nature the right to possess property as his own. . . . It is the mind, or the reason, which is the chief thing in us who are human beings. It is this which makes a human being human, and distinguishes him essentially and completely from the brute. And on this account — namely, that man alone among animals possesses reason — it must be within his right to have things not merely for temporary and monetary use, as other living beings have them, but in stable and permanent possession; he must have not only things which perish in the using, but also those which, though used, remain for use in the future.[13]

Many of the present economic ills of society may be attributed to the selfish possession and accumulation of property by the few, the rich, and too little possession by the vast majority, the poor. The former, for the most part, are included individually or collectively under the term "capitalism." The latter are usually designated "propertyless wage earners." By the beginning of the twentieth century, the effects of the industrial revolution, with its new methods of large-scale production and distribution of goods, were seen in most nations. As a consequence, in the world of economics, society gradually became divided into two groups or classes, namely, capital and labor. The

---

[13] Leo XIII, *Rerum Novarum, op. cit.,* p. 170.

capitalistic class, few in number, secured for themselves a disproportionate measure of worldly goods through the accumulation of wealth. They enjoyed a high standard of living by their possession of the luxuries created by scientific research and invention. The laboring class embraced the multitude of workers who were dependent for their subsistence on occupational opportunities provided by industry, or made possible by capital invested in various productive enterprises. The so-called "iron law of wages," namely, that the cost of production and the selling price determine what is paid for services, was applied with the result that labor received only a small part of the returns. Capital demanded so great a return on its investment that what actually was paid in wages kept the laborer reduced to a veritable state of poverty. The standard of living necessarily was low, so low, indeed, that many persons found it impossible to secure for themselves and their families the necessary food, shelter, and clothing required for subsistence. This class, for the most part, found it impossible to acquire property, because all the wages derived from laboring as many hours as they could endure physically and still produce with efficiency, were barely enough to provide the immediate necessities of life.

Capital, to a large degree, condoned this state of affairs with the specious argument that it was the inevitable consequence of the operation of economic laws. The alleviation of human suffering, therefore, was left to the religious and charitable agencies. This grave violation of distributive justice was upheld, in certain instances, by legislative enactments which prohibited the laborer from seeking redress for his wrongs. Labor gradually rebelled against these conditions, began to organize, and employed the strike as a weapon against the oppressions and injustices of capitalism. Under the influence of false counsels, however, and the erroneous socialistic philosophy advocated by certain leaders, labor clamored, in some instances, for the whole of the profits. In these instances, therefore, by the misuse of its right to organize, and by the denial of the principles of social justice, labor sought to exclude capital from its just share of the profits, and thereby threatened the very stability of the economic and social structure.

Pius XI recognized this state of affairs and set forth the solution as follows:

Now, not every kind of distribution of wealth and property among men is such that it can at all, and still less can adequately, attain the end intended by God. Wealth, therefore, which is constantly being augmented by social and economic progress, must be so distributed among the various individuals and classes of society that the common good of all, of which Leo XIII spoke, be thereby promoted. In other words, the good of the whole community must be safeguarded. By these principles of social justice one class is forbidden to exclude the other from a share in the profits. This sacred law is violated by a wealthy class who, as it were carefree in their possessions, deem it a just state of things that they should receive everything and the laborer nothing.

It is violated also by a propertyless wage-earning class who demand for themselves all the fruits of production, as being the work of their hands. Such men, vehemently incensed against the violation of justice by capitalists, go too far in vindicating the one right of which they are conscious; they attack and seek to abolish all forms of ownership and all income not obtained by labor, whatever be the nature or function these represent in human society, for the sole reason that they are not acquired by toil. . . .

Each one, then, must receive his due share, and the distribution of created goods must be brought into conformity with the demands of the common good, that is, of social justice. For every sincere observer is conscious that the vast differences between the few who hold excessive wealth and the many who live in destitution constitute a grave evil in modern society.[14]

The Church seeks to effect economic democracy in the social order through the extension and wider distribution of ownership of property by the individual. This means the correct application of democratic principles in the social and economic order, but it does not imply that labor should dominate or control capital or industry, for such is communism. Nor does it mean that capital should dominate labor and consider it a commodity subject to the inevitable laws of supply, demand, and price. It does mean, however, that the laborer possesses the right and duty to satisfy his economic needs by earning a living with that same freedom and equality implied by his status as a citizen in a democracy which recognizes and gives maximum expression to all his inalienable rights. Man's political freedom ought to safeguard and augment his economic freedom. His right to vote under political democracy corresponds to his right under economic democracy to obtain a living wage and maintain a normal standard of living. When these latter are provided, the individual can acquire property; and property is the economic means to secure and maintain freedom. It is the safest guarantee against tyranny.

The Church teaches that economic freedom for all

---

[14] Pius XI, *Quadragesimo Anno, op. cit.,* pp. 198–199.

may be had when both capital and labor share in the profits, management, and ownership of industry. By a share in the profits is meant that, after all reasonable deductions have been made for wages, cost of materials, operational expenses, and dividends on investments, some division of the remaining capital gains be made in which labor will share. It should be emphasized that sharing in profits cannot be considered a compensation for low wages, nor should it serve to enslave the laborer to industry. It should, on the contrary, make him a partner, as it were, in the industry, and stimulate his interest in the success of the business which he has helped to create through his labor. The Church suggests that labor ought to participate with employers in the management of those things which are of mutual concern to each; for example, working conditions and hours of employment, wages, seniority rights, pensions, vacations, etc. When such participation takes place both employer and employee benefit. Workers take greater interest and pride in the efficient operation and prosperity of the business; employers usually experience increased production, larger profits, and a stronger "peace of mind" against strikes, work stoppages, carelessness, and sabotage.

The Church further suggests that labor share, to however small extent, in industrial ownership. This does not imply that the worker should become a co-proprietor in the business; rather, it means that the worker is entitled to a share of the profits, products, or values which he helps to produce. This share in ownership should take such form as to assure the laborer some financial return over and beyond his wages, so that his efforts and interests in the success of the business are the same as would be found, normally, in the case of his own personal property.

True democracy cannot be effected in the social order so long as economic autocracy exists. Capital cannot exist without labor, and labor likewise requires capital. Both must be governed by the eternal norms of the moral law. When they conform to this law, economic democracy becomes a reality, and freedom is placed on a firm economic and social foundation.

3. PHILOSOPHICAL. Within the past quarter century, certain exclusive philosophical notions of democracy have attained significant proportions in the United States. These express in a somewhat positive and seemingly authoritative manner the principles of democracy, but, in the main, they present varying and frequently contradictory interpretations and applications of these principles. It is patent that many individuals have been influenced by these exclusive and erroneous notions, and, in turn, seek to implement democratic principles and practices in a manner that is not in conformity to the teachings of true philosophy and revelation. Obviously, any attempt to actualize the Four Freedoms under a false and exclusive interpretation of democracy is certain to result in failure.

Brief consideration will now be given to three of these philosophies, namely, experimentalism, neorealism, and idealism, expressed respectively by Dewey, Breed, and Horne. Each envisages democracy as a way of life; not the Christian way of life, but, rather, one patterned after the specific interpretation given by a particular philosophy to the fundamental principles of democracy.

1. EXPERIMENTALISM. The exponents of experimentalism assert that it alone can correctly interpret democracy and its underlying principles. This philosophy proclaims its ability to direct unfailingly the course of democracy in the reconstruction of the social order. Its chief contributors have been Pierce, James, and Dewey. At the present time, John L. Childs is its leading interpreter and exponent.

In the United States, experimentalism is considered synonymous with the philosophy of John Dewey.[14a] According to that philosophy, democracy is "an inclusive way of life"; in reality, the *experimental* way of life. It is founded on a continuous remaking and refinement of experiences, beliefs, and standards. It is held to be the "intelligent" substitute here on earth for a future heaven. Experimentalism holds that everything is in a state of flux and subject to constant change: man, the world, morality, democracy, freedom, and their every expression. All of these must, therefore, be conformed to the "tested and accepted thought products of science" and to the scientific method. Any notion of democracy which excludes *constant change* as its basic tenet is entirely rejected. Experience and "reconstructed experiences" provide the only means to know and apply, with any degree of certainty, the principles and practices which characterize the democratic way of life.

Dewey professes respect for individuality, but holds that the dignity and worth of the individual mean very

---

[14a] Cf. Smith, M., *John Dewey and Moral Education* (Washington, D. C.: Guthrie Lithograph Co., 1939); O'Connell, G., *Naturalism in American Education* (New York: Benziger Bros., 1938); Redden, J. D., and Ryan, F. A., *A Catholic Philosophy of Education* (Milwaukee: The Bruce Publishing Co., 1942), pp. 476–536.

little unless it is recognized that man is "continuous with nature." As such, man is nothing more than a "highly cultivated and developed organism," differing from the lower animals in degree but not in kind. Man, then, is viewed as a biological organism, who, because of his high state of evolutionary development, can undergo a "humane experience." He is dependent entirely on his social environment, possesses no spiritual origin or principle of life, is a product of evolving matter, and has no "fixed end" apart from this world and the service of the group. The goal of man, which is entirely social, is attainable through a continuous reconstruction of, and growth in, *experience*. Dewey emphasizes this when he writes, "Nothing is relative to growth save more growth."

It is clear that Dewey's philosophy excludes the true democratic principle which upholds the worth and dignity of the individual. Such exclusion denies man's divine origin, destiny, his nature as affected by original sin, his inalienable rights from the Creator, and the moral law existing outside of and beyond the will of society. It follows from this exclusive view of the worth and dignity of the individual that, under the philosophy of experimentalism, the Four Freedoms can receive neither correct interpretation nor adequate expression.

The second principle of true democracy, namely, that society exists for man, not man for society, is interpreted by Dewey in the following manner. Man exists for society and has no individual or life purposes other than those accorded him as a member of society. His sole purpose is to serve society and, by the promotion of the social good, to be absorbed by and merged into the social organism. Anything of benefit to society is considered morally good, and anything harmful to society is morally bad. In so far as society benefits and progresses, so does the individual. Since society is constantly changing, and since the individual must interact with his social environment in order to effect rapid adjustments to social changes and new group practices, he must undergo a continual process of conditioning, or, as it is commonly termed, "reconstruction of experience." It is clear, then, that experimentalism excludes the true meaning and application of this second democratic principle, namely, society exists for man.

Dewey denies any supernatural origin of freedom and authority derived from man's Creator, and founded on the moral law. In fact, Dewey denies both the existence of God and the moral law. He holds that the universe and all in it change continuously; and, hence, that any concept of freedom and authority must be governed by this notion of change. In order to guide and direct the course of change, to reconstruct experience according to the group pattern, and to effect necessary adjustments required by society, some means of control must be employed. This control, commonly designated as authority, is, according to Dewey, an expression of the stability of the social unit from which the individual receives direction and support. Freedom within that social unit designates the operation of those forces by which change is intentionally produced and to which the individual must become adjusted. Thus, for Dewey, organized group intelligence provides the control, and grants the liberties of expression; it is the source of all freedom and authority. Through the operation of this intelligence, the individual experiences the "felt need" for freedom and authority as essential and instrumental to his effective interaction and integration with society. Of course, the social group determines the limits governing the exercise of such freedom and authority; and through the reconstruction of experiences and changed social conditions those limits are subject to constant modification.

From this it follows logically that man's inalienable rights and their expression are subject entirely to society, the group will. The experimentalist interpretation of this third principle of democracy, namely, that freedom and authority come from God and are governed by His law, while recognizing the need of authority and freedom, is, nevertheless, exclusive and erroneous. Dewey positively denies the existence of God, the moral law, and any supernatural source of authority. By such denial, experimentalism at once disqualifies itself from interpreting democracy in its true meaning, and, furthermore, from any intelligent attempt to account for freedom or to suggest the proper actualization of the Four Freedoms.

According to Dewey, the individual has rights and duties. These are held to be entirely social in their origin and sanctions. They come from the operation of organized group intelligence directed to the solution of problems arising from the attempt to effect social betterment. Rights, say the experimentalists, originate from the pragmatic exercise of social authority, and duties flow from the individual's social obligation.

This fourth principle of democracy is falsely interpreted, therefore, by the experimentalists, because they exclude and deny the real origin of and sanctions for all rights and duties. If the source of man's rights resides in the group, or in society as a whole, as experimentalism holds, then, man possesses no *inalienable* rights. What society can grant, society can take away. Likewise, if man defines his own duties as he pleases, or as the group pleases, then, these duties are associated with no final, ultimate sanction, and hence may well be regarded lightly by those who choose so to regard them.

Dewey accepts the fact that there is both equality and inequality among individuals. In physical and mental capacities they are unequal. They are equal, however, by virtue of the fact that each possesses an individuality, a personality of his own, as it were, "the manifestation of something irreplaceable." This means that every person can undergo "humane experiences." Since society is held to be the source of all authority, then, the accepted, tested good of the greatest number, namely, the majority, rules and has authority over the minority. The majority, in itself, is held to be supreme.

It ought to be obvious that the principles of true philosophy must govern and correctly interpret the concepts of "equality" and "majority rule," since all men have *inalienable* rights and are equal in the eyes of their heavenly Father. Thus, equality and majority rule must, perforce, be interpreted according to their proper meaning and limitations. Unless this democratic principle is correctly interpreted and applied, the Four Freedoms can never be rightly envisaged nor properly exercised.

While experimentalism affirms, in the main, the basic principles of democracy, nevertheless it interprets them in an exclusive way. For that very reason, therefore, the democratic way of life cannot be constructed and maintained according to this philosophy.

2. NEOREALISM. A second positive, but exclusive, interpretation of the principles underlying the democratic way of life is found in the philosophy of neorealism. This modern form of realism arose partly as a reaction against the extreme views of experimentalism with its consequent "progressive" tendencies, and has taken the form of "essentialism." Its chief exponent is F. S. Breed, who has set forth the best systematic treatment of it in his book entitled *Education and the New Realism*.[15] This philosophy holds that external objects, *realia*, rather than ideas, constitute reality. In other words, real things exist independent of so-called mental patterns or phenomena. Reality, then, is that which exists objectively. Truth is what reality is purported to be; it is judged by the degree and the extent to which it corresponds to reality. In this matter of correspondence, scientific truth is implied. In the words of Lodge, "Reality, for the modern realist, is, roughly, the content of the physical sciences."[16] It is the eternal manifestation of matter as evidenced by "emergent evolution." By "emergent evolution" is meant that real things, realities, rise out of changes resulting from continually evolving matter. The individual must be alert to recognize these realities and conform his thought and action to them. Whenever ideas become actualized and work in practice, it is only because they conform to reality.

---

[15] Breed, F. S., *Education and the New Realism* (New York: The Macmillan Co., 1939).

[16] Lodge, R. C., *Philosophy of Education* (New York: Harper and Brothers, 1937), p. 6.

When applied to scientific research, realism teaches that the object around which research centers always has specific physical reality in itself, and, as such, can be perceived quite readily. Mind and its operation is but another manifestation of matter. Knowing is simply a relationship "into which things enter" with the various physical and mental aspects intersecting and converging on one another in perception or consciousness.

It is plain that neorealism is another form of materialistic monism. It positively denies God, the existence of a spiritual soul, and the freedom of the will. It recognizes, moreover, no distinction between spirit and matter. Like experimentalism, it considers man as superior to the animals, differing from them in degree but not in kind.

What interpretation is given by neorealism to the principles of democracy? This philosophy views man in a purely materialistic manner, as a product of emergent evolution. His conduct must be constantly conditioned and modified according to behavioristic patterns and methods in order that he may better interact with his social environment. According to Lodge " . . . realism regards the individual as so much nervous tissue . . . in interaction with the physical environment."[17] Man's nature, then, is held to be entirely physical and material. His origin is attributed to the forces of emergent evolution. His end is no higher than that of the world in which he lives, and this end is what every material creature strives to attain, namely, the best possible social adjustments, and the

---

[17] Lodge, R. C., *op. cit.,* p. 70.

maximum satisfaction of human needs. In other words, the individual exists solely to effect necessary adjustments between himself and his constantly changing environment, to the end that he may promote social welfare and satisfy his material wants.

Breed holds that society exists to serve the needs of its members. The societal form required to serve these needs best must embrace a realistic and objective view of the functions both of the individual and of society. This form should be based largely on the results of scientific investigation and experimentation, not on the teachings of philosophy. While philosophy is helpful, according to Breed, it is not the foundation on which society should be based.

Neorealism denies any supernatural origin of freedom or authority. It attributes the source of these entirely to the social forces of environment. Individual liberty and authority are both recognized as essential, but are considered wholly social in origin and purpose. Present in the environment and the social heritage are certain determinants which serve to condition and bring the individual into conformity with the socially desirable exercise of freedom and submission to authority. Realism opposes certain radical experimental procedures which deny the importance of discipline and the systematic influence of the mature mind over the immature, and which urge that the individual choose his own truth and respond only to "felt needs." Breed, representing neorealism, holds that both individual and social interests must be respected. Freedom must always be supplemented by appropriate authority which enforces a necessary discipline on the individual, and is essential to his successful participation in social living and for meeting the conditions of social change. Since the source of freedom and authority, according to neo-realism, is a materialistic, mechanistic environment, such a philosophy cannot, for that very reason, correctly interpret either democracy or freedom, nor can it offer the true concept of the democratic way of life, properly so called, wherein the Four Freedoms may find their appropriate expression.

Realism places the source of all rights and duties within the natural order, and emphasizes the importance of man's social duties. Both the individual and society have rights and duties with respect to each other, but the sanctions for these "rest on the demands of the world without."

By denying the true source and sanctions for rights and duties, the philosophy of neorealism excludes the true meaning and application of that democratic principle which positively asserts that all rights and duties have their origin and sanction from God.

Breed advances no data relative to the equality of man which truly recognize the only basis on which equality can be interpreted. He denies the common origin of all men in God, and their ultimate destiny as eternal salvation — truths which correctly and intelligently interpret man's equality. Again, neorealism presents an erroneous view of "majority rule," for the reason that freedom and authority, on which majority rule must be based, are denied a moral foundation.

It should be concluded that neorealism presents a one-sided, exclusive interpretation of the principles of democracy governing man, society, freedom and author-ity, rights and duties, equality, and majority rule. Some of these principles are, on the surface, upheld and supported; yet, the erroneous philosophical interpretations which neorealism offers, render any correct application to democratic living impossible. It must be concluded, therefore, that the Four Freedoms cannot be expressed completely and correctly under the exclusive views of the new realism.

3. IDEALISM. This philosophy may be traced to certain thinkers in ancient Greece. With the passing of centuries, it has assumed various forms. Applied to education in the United States, its chief exponent, at the present time, is Herman Harrell Horne. Idealism is usually given two distinct meanings: first, an affirmation of certain ideals and values interpretative of the immaterial; second, a metaphysical view of reality and of the ordering principle governing reality. It is the latter meaning that has received greatest application. In the modern form of idealism two types should be distinguished: (1) absolute idealism, which interprets reality in an impersonal manner. A universal mind is held to order the universe. This mind, which constitutes the substance of all things and represents the perfection of all individual minds, is termed the *Absolute*. The existence of God and man herein are merged into one all-inclusive consciousness. (2) Personal idealism, which asserts that the realities and values of life are found in the experiences and purposes of persons. God is considered "the greater person," "the self of selves." Freedom is man's power of self-determination. Immortality is the destiny to which man aspires with "the Author of life." Personal idealism opposes materialism, naturalism, and positivism, by emphasizing man's worth and dignity, his

free will, his ethical ideals as worthy of pursuit and development. Human personalities are viewed as "developing images of the Divine Personality."

Horne is a personal realist, and, with certain reservations, may be described as a spiritual monist, that is, one who tends to submerge man into a spiritual Absolute. The discussion of idealism in this chapter is limited to those aspects of Horne's philosophy which are concerned with the interpretation of the principles of democracy.

Dewey's philosophy was shown to be one of *change;* Horne's, on the contrary, is one of *being.* Horne holds that there are unchanging realities which always go on existing in the world. These are concepts, essences, and universals. The conceptual order, then, is changeless. There is a perceptual order, however, which changes. Idealism, therefore, gives recognition to the permanent and to the changing. While Horne speaks of God, yet, from the vagueness and obscurity of his writings, in certain instances, he seems to display pantheistic leanings. These apparent leanings, however, are vehemently denied by his many students. It is true that he espouses certain of the teachings of Jesus Christ, particularly those which definitely oppose materialism, skepticism, agnosticism, and pantheism. He holds that man and nature are in God, and not God in nature. This belief is commonly termed idealistic theism. This theism admits, moreover, the existence of matter as external to the mind. Horne, therefore, seems to recognize the existence of dualisms in the world, between God and man, matter and spirit, mind and reality. He seeks, however, to merge such dualisms "in the thought of a spiritual monism, in which God is the constant cause of the world and of its changing processes."[18]

With regard to man's nature, Horne affirms that man is divine in origin, and possesses a body and a spirit. It is because of the spiritual principle that man is considered to have infinite worth, and to be superior in kind to the animals. His end is immortality which implies some kind of absorption into the Absolute Being.

It may be asked at this point: How does idealism interpret the principles of democracy? With regard to the worth and dignity of the individual, Horne avers that man is superior in kind to the lower forms of life and destined for God. Because of what seems to be a pantheistic merging of man with God, the effectiveness of Horne's emphasis on the worth of the individual is weakened to the extent that, it may truly be said, the full and complete implication of the concept *man*, as a free, independent being, is lost.

Horne's interpretation of society and its nature is founded on a strong appreciation of the fact that the individual is a rational personality, whose individuality must be recognized and promoted by society. This does not imply any mechanistic notion of society; rather it recognizes the need for the socialization of the individual as essential to social progress. Thus, society needs to be individualized and the individual needs to be socialized. The former produces leaders, while the latter results in loyal and efficient followers and citizens. Both are recognized as essential for a progressive social order. Horne seeks to solve the antinomy between the

---

[18] Horne, H. H., *The Philosophy of Christian Education* (New York: F. H. Revell Company, 1937), p. 43.

individual and society by Christianity, which he considers both individual and social, as the following passage attests:

Jesus does not think of men as isolated individuals: there are no such. Neither does He think of man as a society without individuality, composed only of regimented individuals. . . . Rather He thinks of man as being in society, and of society as consisting of individualized men, and of this whole society of men as in idea, not yet in fact, exemplifying the will of God.[19]

Idealism definitely teaches that man is free, and that the source of his freedom is God. Freedom is given man for the purpose of carrying out God's plan, yet, this does not mean that man is predetermined in his actions. The reason is because man possesses freedom of choice, and, hence, can respond to material influences and stimuli in a manner that is either good or bad. Man, then, is not forced to conform to his physical or social setting, but rather is morally free to respond to conditions about him or to change them. This freedom, according to Horne, is not absolute; on the contrary, it must be exercised with reason and proper restraint. Authority must be true, for the acceptance of false authority means the loss of freedom. The right use of authority not only tends to perfect the individual personality, but also contributes to the attainment of the ideal society. The individual, therefore, must submit to that authority which is designed to give expression to his legitimate purposes; and, on the other hand, authority must tolerate individual interests and respect accidental social changes. In order that authority fulfill its proper function, it must originate in God.

---

[19] Horne, H. H., *op. cit.*, p. 87.

Thus, idealism accepts God as the source of freedom and authority, and thereby ascribes to them a moral foundation.

Horne, as in his interpretation of freedom and authority, attributes the source of rights and duties to God. He fails, however, to define carefully and to limit the exercise of social authority concerning some of man's rights. He emphasizes that both man and society have rights and claims concerning each other. To exercise these rights, discipline is essential; hence, due sacrifice of certain interests by both the individual and society must be effected. Horne asserts that, in certain instances, notably concerning labor, sanitation, civil laws, the state may restrict the individual's freedom and check the exercise of his rights in the interest of establishing an ideal society.

Horne holds, furthermore, that all men are equal as persons, but not, of course, in abilities. Each individual is to receive, however, appropriate opportunities for personal advancement. This does not mean the same treatment for everyone, but, rather, what is best for each person according to his or her abilities. In this manner, leaders will be developed, and good and efficient followers will result. "Majority rule," for Horne, implies a political device and nothing more. This is because God is recognized as the source of all authority, and the exercise of legitimate authority does not imply that the majority are not bound by the injunctions of the moral law in their rule over the minority.

It should be recognized that the philosophical teachings of Horne's idealism are, in the main, in agreement with the truly Christian interpretation of the principles of democracy. The worth and dignity of the individual are recognized and upheld, despite Horne's obscurity in presenting a clear and exact interpretation of man's supernatural origin and destiny. It is true, however, that idealism postulates this supernatural origin and destiny; but it fails to substantiate it by sound logic and an appeal to fundamental truths. The views set forth relative to the nature of society, freedom and authority, equality, and majority rule, agree fundamentally with the true interpretation of the principles of democracy. A somewhat exclusive interpretation is given by Horne, however, to man's inalienable rights and their full and correct exercise.

Strictly considered, idealism, in its interpretation of the principles of democracy, is incomplete and exclusive. It fails to recognize the true relationship existing between God and man, the true nature, purpose, and destiny of man, the true concept of the soul. All of these can be known with certainty only through the teachings of right philosophy which is buttressed by the infallible truths of divine revelation. While idealism is an approach to truth, and offers substantial support to the exact interpretation of the principles of democracy, yet, it is incomplete. Hence under such a philosophy, excluding as it does the truths of divine revelation and right philosophy, the Four Freedoms can hardly attain full and complete expression.

FREEDOM UNDER DEMOCRACY. The democratic way of life cannot be restricted to political, economic, social, or exclusively philosophical aspects. If democracy is to receive full expression and application, it must embrace a right interpretation of man's dignity and worth, his inalienable rights and duties, the meaning of freedom, authority, society, equality, and majority rule.

Man's rights are not merely political, economic, or social; they are truly moral rights, and imply moral obligations which must be discharged. Freedom under democracy truly means the ability to do what one ought to do in conformity with his rational nature, and with the Christian principles which govern all individual and social conduct. This means, on the part of the individual, submission to that lawfully constituted authority which is designed to promote the common temporal welfare of society. It means also that this authority must, at the same time, uphold the worth and dignity of the individual and defend his inalienable rights.

Now, this fact should be emphasized, namely, that there can be no true democracy in the Christian meaning of the term, when freedom and authority are exclusively and erroneously interpreted. Thus, the democratic way of life requires that *freedom* be correctly defined as a gift from God, inalienable and inviolable on the part of any authority or power on earth.

Again, it should be iterated that there can be no true democracy when any *one* of the Four Freedoms is excluded or denied. To deny one of them is to deny them all. They are all integrally related, and the exclusion of any one produces the collapse of the entire democratic structure. While man may be said to enjoy political freedom, economic freedom, nevertheless, if religious freedom is denied him, there is no democracy, but rather aristocracy, autocracy, despotism, or some form of totalitarianism. Freedom of worship, then, is of prime importance. Upon this freedom rests the success or failure of the other three freedoms and the fate of democracy. If freedom of speech and expression, freedom from fear, freedom from want, are not founded upon freedom to worship God according to the dictates of conscience, then, such freedoms lose their vitality and sanction, and become merely liberties bestowed outwardly by the state. As such, if the state can grant, so can the state withdraw when conditions appear expedient.

The question is often raised: "How can this democratic way of life be extended to include every person in the United States and in the world at large?" It can be extended when a correct interpretation of democracy and its component Four Freedoms is accepted, presented, and implemented by right education. The individual, therefore, must be thoroughly indoctrinated in those moral-religious standards governing all truth, goodness, and beauty. These standards are supplied with authority and certainty by divinely revealed religion, and not by science. Gauss emphasizes the futility of the attempt to improve the goodness of the individual by science alone in the following passage:

It is an illusion then for scientists to believe that the application of their methods can make men better. No matter how much you prolong his life or increase his goods, Adam remains old Adam. Even in the Garden of Eden he wanted more than the Lord felt it safe to give him. He probably always will want more. Science cannot make him better. It can only make him better off. That is all we have a right to expect from the scientist; and so far as the relations of nation to nation and man to man are concerned, at this point someone else must take over.[20]

---

[20] Gauss, C., "Can We Educate for Democracy?" *Bulletin of the American Association of University Professors,* Vol. 28, No. 5, December, 1942, pp. 621–622.

From the analysis of democracy presented in this chapter it is evident that the democratic way of life, which in the United States is commonly described as the American way of life, can never be interpreted as something separate and distinct from the Christian way of life. It is, in truth and fact, nothing more than the application of Christian principles to the life experiences of all men in every aspect of individual and social conduct. These principles must, perforce, govern every expression of democratic theory and practice, if democracy itself is to exemplify the *right* way of life in conformity to the eternal law of God. Education in and for these principles and this law is the only true and effective education for democracy. When these principles or fundamental truths are accepted and applied in individual and social living, it may be said that the democratic way of life truly becomes a reality, and that all the requirements are present for the Four Freedoms to become actualized and flourish in a social order that is essentially Christian.

Chapter IV

IMPLEMENTATION OF FREEDOM

INTRODUCTION. If the individual is to be really free, and adequately fitted to exercise and enjoy the Four Freedoms, the truths on which those freedoms rest must become a part of him, and must serve as norms to govern his conduct. "You shall know the truth, and the truth shall make you free."[1] Since the individual comes into this world in a state of helplessness and dependence, he needs the sympathetic but firm influence of the mature mind of the adult so that he may know these necessary truths, learn to cherish them, and make them function in his daily living. This is only another way of saying that man's intellect and will, the highest powers of his rational nature, need enlightenment, discipline, and guidance through what is known as "formal education." It is commonly agreed, among educators in the United States at least, that this *formal* education is the cornerstone of democracy, the democratic way of life, and the Four Freedoms. This is not to say that any type of education can serve as a means to this end. Rather, only *right* education, flowing from true philosophy, can fulfill this high purpose.

---

[1] John, 8:32.

Few men have set forth this fundamental fact with as cogent thought as Father Bernhardt in the following passage:

Each individual human being has a right to an adequate education. He has a right to knowledge, a right to know the truth and the truths. An educated Catholic knows things: things that are grand things to know: There are Three Persons in One God, Christ is in the Sacrament of the Altar; things that are happy things to know: Mary is the Mother of God and Immaculate; things that are sorry things to know: that each single human being starts life handicapped by guilt of his nature: stained and blotted and marked by original sin; that an eternal pain awaits in another world the soul that departs from this in unpardoned sin; things that are consoling things to know: that Baptism cleanses away the primal stain: that Christ is the atoning Redeemer of the whole race.

The individual has a right to be recognized as such. Individual worth is recognized by Catholic education, for each and every human being is thought of as God's individual creation, each one in a state of grace is looked upon as an individual child of God, to whom God individually gives, whom angels individually guard. The Church educates her educators to be fosterers of God's children and busy stewards of their separate heritage.

Full, complete, true education faces the facts of supernatural religion, and basing its philosophy upon an acceptance of Original Sin, a remembrance of Sanctifying Grace, it is safe, it is sound; it sees man as individual, as social, as a unit member of a unit family, as a unit citizen of a unit state, as a unit member of a unit Mystical Body of Christ, and exercising its ministry of education in the light of these considerations, that education is rounded, it is perfect.

The educated Catholic will have a right to know his religion for a thing revealed of God, his Church for a Church of divine founding; he will have a right to a knowledge and a use of the sacraments and the sacramentals; he will have a right to an alert assertion of dogma, to believe it on God's say so; he will have a right to an illuminated intellect, a sanctified understanding, a supernatural wisdom. And he has his educative right to all the prudence gained through his education from the moral teachings imparted by his instructors. Reason and religion warn of a nature prone to evil, a body that leans to lust, a soul that soars to pride. The formative years of puberty, the plastic age of adolescence have their perils and their problems. Solutions of the problems, safeguarding from the perils — no little part of education's task is here. Youth will accordingly have the right to a training of character, to moral instruction and guidance so that he may set up dykes against the unruly swell of passion, may curb in check the rebelling upsurge of pride, may keep mind dominant over flesh, and his human reason subordinate to divine revelation.

And the educated being will have his right to freedom, then: the freedom of the children of God; all freedom that comes of an enlightened intellect, all liberty that a controlled will generates. His will be a placid realization of a free power over controlled inclinations. That freedom comes of an education that takes full cognizance of the nature of man and directs all its endeavors to the right unfolding of powers physical, intellectual, moral, situated in the immortal soul. The enjoyed exercise of these rights the family, the state, and the Church must respect and guarantee.

The end of it all, the completed education which the Church envisages, which she acts on as her aim, pursues as her purpose, is life, abundant life, not here so much as hereafter, a life achieved and won, a membership in a society, in a kingdom, a society of saints, the kingdom of God; vision supernal of God supernal, companionship with Mary and the Blessed; happiness not incidental or accidental, but essential; the end to which the means lead, for which the means are proffered: a clean, healthy body for the sake of the pure risen one; a withering wealth for the purchase of fadeless substance; a little knowledge for the greatest of knowings; power for its pregnant possibilities of good.

Certainly, the Church would have us gentlemen, scholars, saints. We fail of the highest for the ideal is sublime; we proceed haltingly, the way is rough. The going is arduous and we may faint, but the Church cherishes for our memory the lives of her holy ones who strove and struggled and won and she sets them before us for encouragement and inspiration; for them, for us, for all, the Church points out the exemplar Christ for imitation and following.[2]

In the foregoing passage may be found the meaning and substance of the fourteen truths of philosophy enumerated in Chapter II, which are the bases of all freedom. These truths, likewise, are fundamental for the implementation of the Four Freedoms because from them are derived the following principles governing the nature and purpose of education: (1) Education is an individual and a social process comprising the development, discipline and guidance of all man's powers *according to their proper order, man's true nature, and the right purposes of society.* (2) The purpose of education is to enable man to live "the good life" here on earth, and to attain the end of his creation, namely, happiness with his Creator. This end may be reached, in part, through each of the following: adequate knowledge of the fundamental truths of life; an intellect trained to discern truth, and conformed to the infallible teachings of religion; a firm adherence to moral principles by an enlightened and disciplined will which has acquired the virtue of interior self-control; a knowledge of man's rights and duties, both individual and social; a strong conviction of man's ability to solve his prob-

---

[2] Bernhardt, C. L., "The Idea of Catholic Education," *The Pilot* (Boston), Vol. 114, Nov. 16, 1943, p. 8.

lems in an orderly and peaceful way, which means without recourse to physical violence; a reverence for truth, goodness, beauty, and freedom, in their correct meaning; a vocational preparation which enables man to earn a satisfactory living according to his legitimate purposes, thereby contributing to his own and to society's advancement.

It is the purpose of this chapter to set forth the meaning of right education, and demonstrate why such education is necessary for the implementation of the Four Freedoms. It will be shown, moreover, that such implementation, to be concretely effected, requires a social order constructed on truths which sustain the democratic way of life, for only under that way of life can those freedoms have full expression. That way of life requires a complete explanation of reality in all its aspects, so that neither man, society, morality, democracy nor freedom can be misinterpreted by anyone who is willing to seek and abide by the wisdom found therein.

UNIVERSALISM. The complete explanation of man and his world is usually described by the term "universalism." This term designates a uniform application to every phase of reality of the fundamental principles governing all creation. Thus, universalism recognizes the essential relationship between the supernatural and the natural, the Creator and the created, the individual and the social order. It acknowledges the rights and duties of each of the societies into which man is born or incorporated, namely, the Church, the family, and the State. Universalism, moreover, envisages man as a being composed of a physical body and a spiritual soul; as an individual endowed with inalienable rights and responsible for his conduct; and as a member of society, owing duties to the State, the Church, the family, and the social group. Universalism also embraces the concept that, through the ties of the social heritage and the social customs of the group to which he belongs, man is connected with the past. He has a definite contribution to make toward the amelioration of the present, and the promotion of the common good in the immediate future, by conforming all conduct to the eternal truths underlying the right interpretation of man and his world. He has the obligation, furthermore, to struggle against the forces of false philosophy which seek the destruction of truth and justice. Finally, universalism sees in man a free personality because he has definite moral responsibilities toward his own soul, his body, his material welfare, his fellow men, and his Creator. In order to meet these responsibilities in full measure, man must exercise the Four Freedoms in their proper meaning and limitation. This exercise of freedom must be consonant with a correct overview of reality and of man's rational nature and final end.

Applied to education, universalism means that every aspect of man's nature, "whole and entire," be taken into consideration. In addition, every humane interest in which man's powers are used to produce knowledge, goodness, additions, and changes in the various elements of civilization and in particular in the more refined of these elements, usually spoken of as culture, comes within the scope of this universalism. That scope embraces, therefore, the actualization of the goals, purposes, values, and vital truths derived from true philosophy and divine revelation. Hence, universalism implies on the part of the educator a correct knowledge of the child, his nature, and final end, as well as of the aims, content, and methods of right education. Such correct knowledge is necessary so that the educator may intelligently assist the individual to acquire that discipline and development needed for the relative perfection of his nature, and for the full knowledge of the rights and duties implied in the Four Freedoms.

Under this universalism, therefore, the Four Freedoms can be implemented only by a program of education which develops and trains all of man's powers harmoniously, giving proper emphasis to each, so that no aspect of his nature is excluded, neglected, or denied. Such an educational program must embrace knowledge of man's true nature, as well as the meaning, limitations, and correct uses of freedom and the Four Freedoms, and must seek to employ those situations and activities which enable those freedoms to function in daily living. To this end, education must go hand in hand with true philosophy, which is its guide and counselor. It is important, therefore, to show now the relationship between philosophy and education.

PHILOSOPHY AND EDUCATION. That body of related, fundamental principles about man and his world which a person accepts for himself as true constitutes his philosophy of life. Thus, a philosophy of life is based primarily on the first principles that one accepts as valid, workable, and that serve as guides for conduct. It is most important that the first principles or ultimate truths, which serve to direct one's life, be true in themselves. If first principles are false, then one's philosophy of life, of necessity, is false.

From a person's philosophy of life, from his "world

view," comes his philosophy of education. A philosophy of life, if it is really a philosophy, sets up certain ultimate, unchanging principles on which a philosophy of education is based. A philosophy of education, in its turn, sets up certain outcomes, goals, purposes, to be attained in relation to those first principles accepted as true. A philosophy of education, then, is made up of those fundamental, guiding principles which direct and govern the training and formation of the child toward certain predetermined and purposeful ends, which have been established beforehand by a philosophy of life.

Since education entails the instruction and training of youth according to a definite pattern, fundamental truths and purposes must be clearly known and kept in view by educators, in order that they may discern whether or not the child is making progress toward the attainment of that definite pattern, and toward those goals which are embraced under the Four Freedoms.

MEANING OF EDUCATION. The word *education* has been given a wide variety of interpretations. At the outset, a distinction must be made between that educational development which a person acquires solely through his own efforts, unaided by any authoritative or formal influence, commonly known as "informal education," and that development, discipline, and training which result, primarily, from the systematic guidance of the mature mind over the immature mind, usually designated as "formal education." In its broad meaning, education embraces the development and training of all man's powers and capacities for their legitimate individual and social uses. In its narrow meaning, education may be limited to the acquisition of selected habits, skills, attitudes, knowledge and appreciations.

The following definition emphasizes the broad meaning of education; and it is with this meaning that the term "education" is used throughout this book.

FORMAL EDUCATION IS THE ORDERLY INFLUENCE OF THE MATURE MIND ON THE IMMATURE MIND, THROUGH THE SYSTEMATIC DEVELOPMENT AND DISCIPLINE OF ALL THE POWERS OF THE INDIVIDUAL, NAMELY, PHYSICAL, SOCIAL, INTELLECTUAL, MORAL, AESTHETIC, AND SPIRITUAL, ACCORDING TO THEIR RIGHT OR PROPER ORDER, SO THAT HE MAY FULFILL HIS LEGITIMATE PURPOSES ON EARTH, AND ATTAIN ETERNAL SALVATION.

It should be emphasized that education for the Four Freedoms must be essentially formal, because indispensable knowledge must be inculcated, necessary habits and skills formed, and right attitudes and appreciations developed. The purpose of formal education is to fit the individual for social and vocational competence here on earth, and assist him to attain his ultimate end.

If the child is to be developed and trained so that he may correctly exercise and enjoy freedom, the work of education must include the following: (1) acceptance and use of intelligent teacher authority; (2) acquisition of knowledge of the social heritage, and of religious truths which govern all individual and social life; (3) obedience to constituted authority so that the individual may overcome his inherent weaknesses through right living; (4) development of all the individual's powers according to their proper order and importance; (5) guidance to enable the individual to be-

come self-reliant and socially competent; (6) opportunity to cooperate with one's fellow men and contribute to the common good; (7) acceptance of the truth
that the individual is not an end in himself, nor a
means to another person's end; and (8) direction of all
man's capacities and achievements to the greater glory
and service of God.

CHILD NATURE. In the implementation of the Four
Freedoms by education, various aspects of that science
must be correctly understood and interpreted. The
most important of these concerns, of course, the
nature of the child, the future citizen who will exercise
and enjoy these freedoms. It is the proper function of
education to teach the child how to make right choices
in conduct, and, with this end in view, to develop and
discipline all his powers according to their right order
and his essential needs. In order that this development
and discipline may be actualized, and those needs provided for, the individual's true nature must be correctly understood. Two basic questions, then, present
themselves: (1) What is the nature of the child who
is the subject of education? (2) How ought the child
to be educated according to his nature?

From philosophy one learns that the child possesses
not only an individual nature but a social nature as
well. From the standpoint of his individual nature, the
child has certain physical, intellectual, moral, aesthetic,
and spiritual needs. From the standpoint of his social
nature, the child is disposed to interact and cooperate
with his companions not only for his own personal
advancement but for the mutual benefit of the group.
To this end, he must learn how to become socially
competent.

Revelation teaches that man was created by God to His image and likeness and is destined for eternal bliss. The child's education, therefore, has as its purpose not only individual and social competence, but, primarily and ultimately, the attainment of his supernatural end. Pure reason, unaided by divine revelation, could never *completely* discover this ultimate destiny provided for man. It is these two truths, namely, man's divine creation and his spiritual destiny, that prove the worth and dignity of the individual human being. These truths must, perforce, govern and condition the entire educative process. In consequence, all proximate ends in education and life, whether individual, social, economic, civic, or vocational, must be subordinated to that ultimate purpose of all striving, namely, man's eternal salvation. Hence, these infallible truths must be known and recognized by the educator himself, first of all, if he would seriously influence and train the child to approach his supernatural end with certainty, and to subordinate appropriately all natural desires and purposes to the attainment of this goal. Revelation makes known, furthermore, that man once enjoyed a state of pristine loveliness, in which all his powers were ordered in conformity to God's will; that man used his own free will to disobey God's command; and that he thus incurred the divine displeasure. Because of this original sin, man lost his pristine loveliness and, as punishment, was deprived of his right to eternal happiness with God and of certain preternatural privileges, namely, bodily immortality and perfect control of appetite. St. Thomas Aquinas describes man's rectitude before the fall as follows:

For this rectitude consisted in his reason being subject to God, the lower powers to reason, and the body to the soul: and the first subjection was the cause of both the second and the third; since while reason was subject to God, the lower powers remained subject to reason. . . . Now it is clear that such a subjection of the body to the soul and of the lower powers to reason was not from nature; otherwise it would have remained after sin; since even in the demons the natural gifts remained after sin. . . . Hence it is clear that also the primitive subjection by virtue of which reason was subject to God was not a merely natural gift, but a supernatural endowment of grace; for it is not possible that the effect should be of greater efficiency than the cause. Hence Augustine says that, *as soon as they disobeyed the Divine command, and forfeited Divine grace, they were ashamed of their nakedness, for they felt the impulse of disobedience in the flesh, as though it were a punishment corresponding to their own disobedience.* Hence if the loss of grace dissolved the obedience of the flesh to the soul, we may gather that the inferior powers were subjected to the soul through grace existing therein.[3]

All men, the Blessed Virgin alone excepted, are born with this original sin on their souls. Its eternal punishment has been satisfied by Christ's redemption, death on the cross, and this sin is removed from the soul of the individual by baptism.

However, the *vulnera naturae* (the wounds of nature) and the deprivation inflicted on man because of original sin remain. Hence, an understanding of them is fundamental to the work of education and to the correct interpretation of the nature of the child. Because of that sin, the child's intellect is less able to attain truth, his will is less able to choose the good, and his nature is more inclined to concupiscence or disorderly

---

[3] St. Thomas Aquinas, *Summa Theologica* (London: Burns, Oates and Washbourne Ltd., 1927), Vol. IV, pp. 317–318.

affections. It should be made clear, however, in contra-distinction to the teachings of Calvinism, that human nature *is not depraved* and that man's actions are not essentially *sinful;* rather, human nature is *deprived* of certain privileges. Father Farrell explains these depriva-tions and the "wounds of nature" in the following passages:

It is also self-evident that the original justice of man was destroyed by original sin. At least it is self-evident that such perfect harmony of subordination of the will to God, and of the lower faculties to the will, no longer exists, and our Faith tells us that the cause of this was original sin. Certainly we have not the preternatural gifts of immortal-ity, freedom from suffering and pain that our first parents enjoyed.

This we must know: nature remains intact and the gifts acquired by nature through grace are lost. What worries us is the inclination to sin, the damage done to man's natural inclination to virtue, the upset caused by original sin to man's inclination to act according to reason, to follow the paths of reason to the goal of reason where hu-man happiness is found.

Theologians teach, quite accurately, that human nature has suffered four wounds: ignornace in the intellect, malice in the will, weakness in the irascible appetite, and con-cupiscence in the concupiscible appetite. The positive side of that teaching is that the prudence, justice, fortitude, and temperance of human nature have been damaged, that all the principles of activity in man are considerably less effi-cient than they were in the beginning of man's career.[4]

It is clear, then, that in the work of education the child's intellect needs enlightenment, his will needs discipline, and his disorderly affections need to be

---

[4] Farrell, W., *A Companion to the Summa* (New York: Sheed and Ward, 1939), Vol. II, pp. 328, 330.

brought under control. Education must emphasize inflexibly the importance of authoritative guidance and the indispensable value of discipline in the development and training of the child, so that he may be led to overcome the inherent limitations of his nature. Father Guthrie stresses the need for guidance and discipline in these words:

The modern idea that the student should be left to his own spontaneous resources and good judgment, that he should be permitted to choose only those courses which interest him, that with a minimum of dogma, instruction or advice, he should be permitted to follow the bents of his own wholly good nature so that he may grow up unhampered by tradition, unwarped by dogma, unimpeded by instruction, untrammeled by guidance, unshackled by any advice from adults or any formation not wisely mapped out by the exigencies of his own adolescent individuality, is a preposterous hypothesis which traces its heavily tainted parentage to Rousseau's Émile. The youth of today more than ever before need guidance and discipline. Stress laid on the life of the body has crushed the life of the spirit; the unruly surge of passions has obscured reason, while reason in turn is rebelling more and more against God.[5]

The child has a nature which functions on two intimately related levels: the somatic level, pertaining to bodily functions; and the spiritual level, relating to spiritual functions. The former, from the standpoint of education, concerns the training of the senses; the latter embraces the enlightenment and discipline of the intellect, the will, the emotions, and the memory. It may be said, then, that the child exists in a state of *potentiality* for development, and that it is the func-

[5] Guthrie, H., "Education for the Christian Individual," *A Philosophical Symposium on American Education* (New York: Fordham University Press, 1941), pp. 148–149.

tion of education to lead the child out of this potentiality into an actuality which approaches, to the maximum degree, a state of final perfection for him. This is, indeed, the goal of education and of life itself.

The answer to the second question, namely, "How ought the child to be educated according to his nature?" flows logically from an understanding of the powers and needs of his nature. It is clear, at once, that child nature is sensory, intellectual, and volitional, and that for each aspect of his nature certain powers are provided. For the physical, the senses exist; for the intellectual, the capacities for thought, reasoning, and judgment provide truth; for the volitional, the power of will seeks the choice of the good among motives. Each power of the child is impelled to seek its proper object in its highest form. Thus, the intellect seeks truth and beauty, the will good. Upon careful reflection it will be evident that beauty, truth, and goodness embrace both the immediate and the ultimate goals of all right education. By his very nature, the child seeks some means to personify beauty, truth, and goodness. This personification is found only and completely in the way of life taught and exemplified in the person of Jesus Christ. He is the aura of all beauty, truth, and goodness, the acme of perfection, and presents completely the only manner of life by which all may enjoy the full measure of freedom.

This brief discussion of child nature sets forth truths which must be taken into account in order that the Four Freedoms may be correctly implemented by education. These truths show that the child has certain inherent limitations; that his senses must be brought to subserve his intellect; that his intellect and will must strive to attain, as far as possible, through discipline and instruction that "rectitude" which man possessed before the fall. Thus, the child, through his capacity to acquire truth and goodness and by the correct use of his freedom, may come to the ultimate and proximate goals of all his striving.

EDUCATIONAL AIMS. A second aspect of the educative process which must be correctly interpreted, in order that the Four Freedoms may be rightly implemented, is educational aims. True philosophy supplies these valid norms which govern proximate and ultimate educational purposes: (1) The ultimate purpose of man is the attainment of everlasting happiness with God. (2) Education seeks the perfecting of the child in all his powers and capacities in so far as such perfection is humanly possible. (3) There are lower or proximate objectives of education which at all times are secondary in character and importance, but are contributory, either directly or indirectly, to fulfillment of the primary objective. (4) These secondary aims must be subordinated and adapted to the primary objective, so that the natural may always subserve the supernatural, and the temporal promote the eternal.

From philosophy it is clear that the ultimate aim of education is one and the same as the final purpose of man's creation. That ultimate educational aim, then, is so to train the child that he will be both equipped and disposed to strive, with constancy and perseverance, for moral perfection by conduct conformed to moral principles. Thus, the ultimate aim of all education, like that of life itself, is supernatural, and to this end all human desires and social purposes must be ordained. This aim is known from two sources: (1) divine revelation, which informs man infallibly that he has a supernatural destiny to which all human action must be directed; and (2) right reason, which proves logically that man has an immortal soul, and that this soul cannot rest satisfied with material happiness but is destined to possess the highest perfection with its Maker. It follows, therefore, that in the full enjoyment of the Four Freedoms, according to their proper meaning and exercise, the individual must pursue with constancy and steadfastness the ultimate goal of his creation so that he may truly say, "For this was I born, and for this came I into the world; that I should give testimony to the truth" (John 28:37).

Some thinkers, contrary to the maxim "first things should be placed first," substitute, for an ultimate aim, a specific worldly objective or a series of objectives, such as knowledge, guidance, experience, culture, habit formation, adjustment, efficiency, citizenship, democracy. Again, false philosophies have emphasized nature, the individual, society, the nation, the proletariat, as the source and ultimate aim of education. In consequence, confusion, conflict, and exclusivism have resulted. In many instances, interpretations of aims have contradicted truth and have failed to consider the proper functions of society as well as the individual in the fulfillment of the purposes assigned to each by the Creator.

In the face of such misinterpretation, the implementation of the Four Freedoms through *right* education is impossible. Freedom itself and the Four Freedoms can be actualized by means of education only when a true interpretation of the ultimate aim of education is accepted and applied. To attain this ultimate aim, certain proximate or secondary aims are useful. These in

themselves contribute to the acquisition of valuable
knowledge, the formation of desirable habits and skills,
the development of right attitudes and appreciations,
all of which facilitate the realization of man's ultimate
purpose. These secondary objectives imply purposeful efforts, on the part of educators, to train the individual for the successful pursuit of his temporal
vocation, to assist him in his striving for material well-
being, and to awaken him to the necessity for the improvement of the social order and the economic welfare of his fellow men. These secondary objectives,
however, must always serve as means to man's *spiritual*
end. From this fact it is patent that health, vocational
efficiency, citizenship, ethical character, avocational interests, worthy home membership, group cooperation,
self-discovery — all desirable outcomes and immediate
objectives of the educative process, the importance of
which everyone recognizes — are secondary objectives.
When specific instruction and practice are directed
to their pursuit, a measurable contribution is made
to the implementation of the Four Freedoms.

EDUCATIONAL AGENCIES. A third aspect of the educative process concerns the proper scope and function
of the various formal educational agencies with which
the child comes in contact. A *formal* agency is one
which by the use of controlled procedure seeks through
influence, discipline, and development of powers to
effect the attainment of specific goals. Thus, the family,
the Church, the State, and the school are the principal
formal educational agencies. Each must contribute its
respective share to the child's total education and the
enhancement of the Four Freedoms. None can be excluded without grave injury to the child in his total

development. There are, of course, numerous informal agencies, such as the playground, radio, newspaper, theater, wherein education occurs indirectly or concomitantly. Since the child acquires information and knowledge from these sources and, sometimes, error and wrong habits, it is clear that every effort should be made to watch over the child in all his informal as well as formal contacts. Systematic instruction, influence, supervision, and guidance by the formal agencies must set up a veritable immunity, so to speak, which will ward off automatically the evils encountered from the informal agencies. This guidance must be continued until the individual reaches maturity, and by adequate training is fitted to pursue his own purposes with some degree of wisdom.

Educational agencies comprise two types: primary and secondary. There are two primary agencies, namely, God and the educand himself. The four principal secondary agencies are: (1) the Church; (2) the family; (3) the State; and (4) the school.

PRIMARY AGENCIES. Through the gift of sanctifying and actual grace conferred on man, God directly affects the content of education as well as the means employed by the individual in securing an education. By sanctifying grace the child forms in himself a supernatural habit which in turn produces a power and an urge to attain truth and goodness. The full fruit of this power and urge is found in the life to come where its final reward is received. Actual grace affects education by supplying the basis for certain motives, inspirations, impulses, which stimulate the practice of virtue. Thus, the action of God as a primary educational agent is seen directly in the grace which God bestows on the child. Moreover, God extends His influence indirectly in the manifold range of personal stimuli, circumstances, environmental conditions, which the individual encounters, and to which, through the beneficence of divine providence, he responds.

It is patent that education also takes place through the individual's own purposeful or even haphazard self-activity. In truth, beneath any educational development whatsoever lies self-activity on the part of the person himself. The educand has been endowed by nature with the necessary powers, and possesses the inalienable right and duty, to educate himself. In the final analysis there can be no education that is not essentially self-education.[6]

Normally, however, the child requires the influence of maturity, discipline, training, and fostering care to guide him in the discharge of his duty of self-education. The secondary educational agencies fulfill this requirement by directing formally the work of self-education and stimulating the individual's own educative activity. Moreover, since freedom implies the ability to do what one *ought*, the child must be led to seek from authority the right course of action in the attainment of truth and goodness, instead of being allowed to follow the bents of his own undisciplined nature. He cannot, through self-activity alone, discover what is right and good; rather, he needs instruction and guidance so that his choice will be consistent with ultimate truth and goodness. Because the work of self-education and the inculcation of right habits, attitudes, and appreciations

---

[6] Cf. St. Thomas Aquinas, *De Magistro,* as translated by Mayer, M. H., *The Philosophy of Teaching of St. Thomas Aquinas* (Milwaukee: The Bruce Publishing Co., 1929), pp. 51–53.

are affected, in great measure, by the formational work of secondary agencies, it is essential that the exact functions and contributions of each agency be understood and utilized to the maximum degree in attempting to implement the Four Freedoms through education.

SECONDARY AGENCIES. The child is born into the family, which is commonly spoken of as "the primary social unit," the stabilizing element of human society. Through the family he is incorporated into the larger societies of Church and State. It is clear, then, that the individual is a member of three societies, two in the natural order, namely, the family and the state, and the third in the supernatural order, namely, the Church, through which men are called to be saved. The Church and the State are *perfect* societies because each possesses in itself all the means necessary for the attainment of the particular purpose for which God created it. The Church, through grace, the sacraments, prayer, and the spiritual goods won for man by the passion and death of Christ, has all the means necessary to guide the individual infallibly to his eternal salvation. The State has at its disposal all the requisites to attain its end, namely, the protection of the individual citizen through fostering care and the promotion of his temporal welfare. The family, on the other hand, is not a perfect society, for it does not possess all the essentials to fulfill its purpose and discharge its obligations to the child, which comprise "the generation and formation of offspring." Thus, it seeks spiritual sanctification for the child from the Church, and depends, in part, on the State for his temporal, material well-being.

1. THE CHURCH. The Church, through the command of Christ, "Going therefore, teach ye all nations

... to observe all things whatsoever I have commanded you,"[7] possesses not only an order but also a first claim to education. This means a pre-eminent right to educate, nourish, and rear souls according to the pattern set forth and exemplified by Christ. Since God granted His Church infallibility when teaching matters of faith and morals, there is implied herein the duty to teach authoritatively concerning the truth or falsity found in the methods and content of all secular branches of learning in so far as these affect morality and the attainment of the individual's final destiny. This duty to teach is not limited to the proper end and object for which the Church exists, but, in addition, embraces every human activity. The Church, therefore, has the duty to protect her children from evils which might result from the pursuit of any particular branch of learning. She possesses, moreover, the obligation to advise and command parents about the form, organization, and content of the school to which their children should be sent. Likewise, the Church has the authority to condemn, and to forbid attendance at schools found harmful to faith and morals. In the exercise of its proper functions the Church is ever mindful of the legitimate rights and duties of the family and the State, and in no way encroaches on or interferes with these rights and duties when each society properly discharges them.

The Church specifically implements the Four Freedoms by teaching the individual that the correct enjoyment of those freedoms can be had only by consistent conformity in conduct to the injunctions of the moral

---

[7] Matt. 28:19–20.

law, the Ten Commandments, and by the acceptance of the way of life taught and exemplified by Jesus Christ. Therein love of God and love of neighbor, the very pillars of all freedom, are set forth as the supreme ideal.

2. THE FAMILY. The family, because it brings the child into the world, is responsible for its care and development. For this responsibility it is especially fitted and disposed by nature and by grace, and possesses an inviolable right and duty to help in the child's education. This right is *primary*. It embraces the obligation to impart religious, moral, intellectual, physical, and civic training, to select the right kind of school, and, likewise, the manner and content of instruction. In order to exercise this right of education, then, it is clear that the family requires the highest degree of stabilization in the social order, and that the Church and the State must contribute every assistance to the maintenance of this stability.

The right of the family is inviolable; yet, it is not an absolute right, but rather an immediate right, because it must subserve the ultimate good of the child as determined by the moral law and man's last end. When the family, through neglect, ignorance, or incompetence, fails in the discharge of religious, moral, and social obligations to the child, such deficiency, in so far as possible, ought to be made up by the Church and the State, with due regard to those factors which come within the scope of the respective spheres of each. This is evident from the fact that the child has an express right to that fostering care and correct guidance, both temporal and spiritual, which comport with the full worth and dignity of human personality and lead to the fulfillment of the purposes ordained for him by the Creator.

The child receives his earliest intellectual, moral, religious, and social training in the atmosphere of the family. Here are learned the basic language habits, the earliest skills, and obedience to constituted authority. Here essential guidance is provided, good example and first religious instruction given, and the earliest evidences of self-assertion and self-control are nurtured and directed. In all these activities, parental love is fundamental, and lays the foundation for the pursuit of all future educational activity in school and in later life. The family is the primary social unit, and the mother is the supreme educator. In the environment of the family are formed the bases for the acquisition of those intellectual, moral, and social virtues which alone render the individual capable of exercising his inalienable rights, and of enjoying his noble heritage of the Four Freedoms.

The welfare of society requires a home that is permeated with a truly religious atmosphere. Herein the mother, through the purity of her own interior life and by her exemplary conduct, strives to influence the child to form virtuous habits, to accept and respect the teachings of properly constituted authority, and to conform in individual and social conduct to the injunctions of morality. In this manner she contributes immeasurably to the purification of society, and seeks its moral and spiritual regeneration through the recovery of a long lost faith in divine providence and by the application of the universal principles of truth and justice. The mother understands the child, its needs, yearnings, and strivings. She knows best how to direct these into worth-while and noble channels. She has a disposition to lead the child in the way he should go, and to teach his trusting heart to know, love, and serve God, to love his neighbor, and to display virtue and character in conduct. These truly are the fruits of mother love, and they are, likewise, the pillars around which society must be reconstructed if the Four Freedoms are to become an actuality.

3. THE STATE. Because of man's inability to develop his capacities alone, supply fully his material wants, and maintain peace among his fellows, a governing authority is required. Thus, the State is a *necessary* society which man is morally bound to maintain. The individual must live in civil society and derive from it that fostering care, peace, and security necessary to the full development and enrichment of his powers in a manner that is at once religious, cultural, moral, and civic.

Like the family and the Church, the State has rights and duties in the education of the child. These concern the promotion of the common good by the protection of citizens in their bodies, possessions, and by the fostering of their material and spiritual well-being. It is clear, then, that the State exists to serve its members, uphold their rights, protect their freedom, and promote the legitimate exercise thereof. To serve its members adequately, the prior rights of the Church and the family must be respected and upheld. Never with justice can legislation be enacted to usurp, control, or deny the full exercise of these prior rights if the State is to fulfill its duty as a perfect society of the natural order by fostering and protecting the true welfare of its members. The State, moreover, never can justly assume to itself the exclusive power and the fitness to regulate or restrict the inherent right of the individual to educate himself, or the family right in that same work of education. The authority of the State rests largely in its right to require parents and the individual to fulfill their duties to the State itself, and to supply them with material aid to facilitate the discharge of these duties. The State may very properly require that no instruction be given which undermines the common good or threatens the stability of the State itself. The State may rightfully demand, furthermore, that the child acquire knowledge and training in social and civic virtues, such as patriotism, justice, honesty, charity, chastity, self-control, and obedience to constituted authority and law.

In addition to the foregoing, the State has the exclusive right to establish and control schools designed to prepare for certain civic duties, such as the administration of public affairs, the maintenance of law and order, the preservation of peace. The performance of these duties requires special aptitudes and preparation for which specialized schools, such as military academies, are necessary. Care must be taken, however, lest the State injure or seek to usurp the rights of the family and the Church by the specious claim that every branch of learning comes within the scope of civic or social education. It is, of course, the duty of the State to provide for all ages and groups that particular civic education which comes within the correct meaning of the term. This implies the promotion of those activities which truly implement the common welfare. Such activities must be regulated by the norms of "moral rectitude," the worth and dignity of the individual, and the rights of the family and the Church, lest they contradict ultimate truth and goodness and inflict grave injustice on the child, the subject of education.

In the work of education considerable overlapping occurs between the functions of the Church and those of the State. The former is concerned with the individual's spiritual destiny; the latter with his material welfare. Ryan and Millar indicate the respective purposes of each society as follows:

Spiritual and moral matters constitute the province of the Church; civil and temporal matters that of the State. The latter has no authority over the administration of the sacraments; the former has nothing to do with the maintenance of the police force. In those borderland subjects which fall under the jurisdiction of both societies, the distinguishing principle is the same. Those phases of a common subject which have a moral or religious character belong to the Church; those which are in their nature and objects temporal are under the authority of the State. Thus, education is the concern of the State in its civil and social aspects, and of the Church in its religious and moral aspects.[8]

Certain modern nations, which are at present governed by false philosophies, deny and even usurp the pre-eminent right of the Church and the primary right of the family to educate. These nations have substituted a form of State education which is exclusive in character, and they have refused to recognize the inherent worth and dignity of the individual and the existence of inalienable rights. The rulers of these nations have made compulsory an educational program designed to fashion the individual according to a predetermined nationalistic or racial pattern, and have sought thereby his

---

[8] Ryan, J., and Millar, M., *The State and Church* (New York: The Macmillan Co., 1937), p. 49.

complete regimentation. It is obvious that such exaggeration and complete misinterpretation of the educational rights of the State can never result in the development of the individual according to his true nature.

When the State promotes through appropriate legislation those measures which truly contribute to the individual's material and spiritual amelioration, subject, of course, to the norms of the moral law, it may be said that the State thus implements the Four Freedoms. Such implementation requires, on the part of the State through education, the development of exemplary citizens, intelligent men of character, socially and morally virtuous, who understand the purposes of the world they are living in, the place and function of freedom in that world, together with their own responsibilities in the larger society of which they are members.

If the Four Freedoms are to be implemented by education, then the legitimate rights of the family and the Church, as well as those of the State, must be recognized and upheld. Any denial of these, and failure to provide opportunity for their exercise, will destroy the very foundation of freedom. The State, indeed, has the duty to promote the correct exercise of freedom through its strict adherence to the truths governing the individual's nature, the moral law, man's last end, and the proper function of authority in civil society. When the State carries out its proper functions, the Four Freedoms come to complete fruition in social life. Likewise, through the correct interpretation of each of the secondary educational agencies, the foundation is laid for the implementation of these freedoms in their true meaning.

4. THE SCHOOL. A fourth secondary educational

agency is the school. Its main purpose is to supplement and complement the work of education already started and still carried on by the home. This means that the school continues the mental, moral, religious, and social training of the home, by an organized program of formal education. This consists of systematic instruction, discipline, and the harmonious development of the child's powers. In no way, however, may it be said that the school is a substitute for the home. There are elements of the child's education which can never be adequately supplied by any source other than the parents themselves. Children need, above all else, the influence, inspiration, and fostering care of parental love and discipline as well as the guidance and example of the family environment. Only at the risk of grave injury to the child can these be dispensed with; nor do they cease when formal school instruction begins. Hence, despite many assertions to the contrary, parental responsibility is not lessened when the child enters school, nor can it be transferred entirely to other persons or agencies. For, if such transfer were possible, the school might become an institution contributing to the breakdown of the home, the disintegration of the family, the denial of the authority of the Church, and the submergence of home and Church within the framework of the State through a form of state socialism.

There are many who believe that the school can and should assume the greater part of the educational activities and duties of the home. They even belittle the importance of the home as an educational agency, and assert that the school, in modern times, supplies all the training formerly recognized as the function of the home. With all due recognition of and respect for

the splendid work the school is doing in fulfilling its
legitimate functions in social life, and admitting its
indispensable contributions to individual and social
progress, nevertheless, it is essential that a few of the
school's intrinsic limitations be recognized.

Through the school, the child is introduced to a
wider environment that offers opportunities for various experiences in a larger group than that afforded by
the home. The child, moreover, must submit to a new
authority an extension of the authority of the home,
and observe disciplinary regulations imposed by the
teacher, all of which have decided advantages. On the
other hand, the child in school is treated as one of a
group, and because of the limited attention which the
teacher can give him, fails to receive that intimate and
selective training, designed to foster his good qualities
and overcome his inherent weaknesses, which formerly
was provided by the home. In view of this limitation,
the need for a continuance of the spirit and method
of home training, and for a degree of "mothering,"
is quite apparent.

Another limitation of the school is seen in the fact
that it must compete as a formal agency with the manifold informal educational influences which solicit the
child's interest, attention, and effort during the time
when he is not under the care of the school. In his out-
of-school hours the child is constantly interacting with
the various stimuli offered by the environment. He is
educated informally by playmates, games, theaters, the
radio, the newspaper, relatives, and people that he
meets. He may respond actively or indifferently to
various niceties or vulgarisms in language; to good or
bad manners; to certain likes, prejudices, and emotional

outbursts; to good or bad example; and to desirable or undesirable practices and influences. Thus the school, since it is in constant competition with numerous undesirable environmental stimuli, needs at all times the unceasing vigilance and active cooperation of parents to supplement its own limited educational influence.

A further limitation of the school is seen in its apparent inability to develop in the individual a degree of moral excellence beyond that which is commonly included under the elusive term "ethical character." This inability is due to the exclusion of specific religious and moral training from the curriculum. Basic virtues, necessary for the individual's interior life as well as for good citizenship, cannot be acquired informally or incidentally with that degree of certainty which is attained by positive, direct methods. These several limitations of the school indicate the need for full cooperation from other educational agencies so that the child, in his total education, may receive that complete development needed for the proper exercise of freedom.

It is an indisputable fact, however, that children are not qualified for adult social life, in all its complex relationships and required adjustments, by family education alone. This results from the fact that the "younger generation must be trained in the arts and sciences for the advantage and prosperity of civil society," and the family lacks the necessary means to provide such training. The school through right organization, administration, curriculum, and methodology, possesses the means to supply a part of this training. It offers the formal content, instruction, and disciplinary training essential to fit him for adult life.

Thus, the school has four distinct advantages: (1) It provides a simplified environment, in that the more difficult and involved features of adult life are removed. (2) It supplies a controlled environment, inasmuch as only the approved knowledge and practices of social life and culture are included. (3) It furnishes a graduated environment, because activities and curricular content are graded in such manner that the child is led by degrees to approach and finally to exemplify those behavior patterns which characterize adult life. (4) It affords a preparatory environment, because instruction is adapted to the interests and vocational capacities of the child so that he may be trained and fitted to make the necessary adjustments required for a higher social and spiritual life.

The child needs to acquire, formally, certain approved knowledge, habits, skills, attitudes, and appreciations. These include, among other things, the mastery of language; correct expression of ideas; effective imaginal and emotional control; accurate thinking, remembering, judging, and reasoning; ability to differentiate between truth and error, goodness and badness. These abilities require sufficient instruction, discipline, and practice, and the school is the agency established by society to achieve these ends. In the ideal organization of the school, a religious atmosphere should permeate the youth's entire training and be the central element in every activity and branch of the curriculum. So organized, the school can serve admirably to implement the Four Freedoms by training and disciplining the individual consonant with his true nature and the purposes of society, as envisaged in the democratic way of life and as ordained by the Creator for the right exercise of freedom.

Thus, President Conant of Harvard University writes:

Neither the mere acquisition of information nor the development of special skills and talents can give the broad basis of understanding which is essential if our civilization is to be preserved. No one wishes to disparage the importance of being "well informed." But even a good grounding in mathematics and the physical and biological sciences, combined with an ability to read and write several foreign languages, does not provide a sufficient educational background for citizens of a free nation. For such a program lacks contact with both man's emotional experience as an individual and his practical experience as a gregarious animal. It includes little of what was once known as "the wisdom of the ages," and might nowadays be described as "our cultural pattern." It includes no history, no art, no literature, no philosophy. Unless the educational process includes *at each level of maturity* some continuing contact with those fields in which value judgments are of prime importance, it must fall far short of the ideal. The student in high school, in college and in graduate school must be concerned, in part at least, with the words "right" and "wrong" in both the ethical and the mathematical sense. Unless he feels the import of those general ideas and aspirations which have been a deep moving force in the lives of men, he runs the risk of partial blindness.

There is nothing new in such educational goals; what is new in this century in the United States is their application to a system of universal education. Formal education based on "book learning" was once only the possession of a professional class; in recent times it became more widely valued because of social implications. The restricted nature of the circle possessing certain linguistic and historical knowledge greatly enhanced the prestige of this knowledge. "Good taste" could be standardized in each generation by those who knew. But, today, we are concerned with a general education — a liberal education — not for the relatively few, but for a multitude.

The primary concern of American education today is not the development of the appreciation of the "good life" in young gentlemen born to the purple. It is the infusion of the liberal and humane tradition into our entire educational system. Our purpose is to cultivate in the largest possible number of our future citizens an appreciation of both the responsibilities and the benefits which come to them because they are Americans and are free.[9]

THE CURRICULUM. A fourth aspect of the educative process is the curriculum. This must be correctly as well as broadly interpreted, and employed according to its proper end, if the Four Freedoms are to be implemented effectively. In order that the aims of education may be attained, and that education itself may perform its proper functions, an organized body of content, termed the curriculum, is needed. The materials of this content must be selected carefully, arranged systematically, and comprise subject matter, experiences, and activities drawn from the social heritage and accepted as essential in training the child to meet individual and social needs.

In meeting these needs, the nature and interests of the individual and of society, each rightly understood, must be given consideration. The individual by his very nature has certain physical needs, such as knowledge, truth, certitude, self-expression, and creative urges; moral needs, such as goodness, self-control, character, moral integrity, discipline, self-sacrifice; aesthetic needs, such as beauty, art, culture, good manners, appreciations, sentiments; spiritual needs, such as prayer,

---

[9] Conant, J. B., *Report of the President of Harvard University to the Board of Overseers 1941–1942* (Published for the Alumni, Cambridge, Mass., 1943), pp. 10–11.

grace, sacraments, spiritual poise, ultimate happiness. These needs must be satisfied mainly through the individual's own spontaneous efforts. This satisfaction is facilitated by the influences and contacts acquired through a carefully planned educational program designed to stimulate purposeful activity on the part of the individual so that he may attain the harmonious development of all his powers according to their proper order.

Society itself likewise has specific needs, to the satisfaction of which the curriculum must contribute. These needs concern the material well-being and common good of all its members; the attainment and maintenance of world peace; the perpetuation of law and order; the adherence to universal moral principles governing liberty, justice, and democracy; the correct exercise and full enjoyment of the Four Freedoms.

The curriculum must be so organized as to include both "secular" and "religious" materials. The former are supplied by the social heritage. The latter come to man through the authority of divine revelation. These materials, taken together, adequately meet social needs in conformity to the nature of the individual and of society. Religious materials provide the guiding norms, the catalyzer as it were, which control not only the content of the curriculum but also the ends for which the curriculum exists.

The curriculum must be planned and constructed to achieve two major purposes: (1) to provide knowledge of fundamental truths, and training in forms of conduct, which rightly interpret and characterize man, society, freedom, and democracy; (2) to meet the needs of individual differences, and to facilitate the making of those adjustments required by the natural law, the social heritage, and legitimate social change.

For the specific implementation of the Four Freedoms, the curriculum must include those fundamental truths on which any valid conception of freedom must be based. Furthermore, the curriculum must embrace definite content, activities, and experiences, designed to insure the acquisition of the correct meaning of the Four Freedoms as well as the proper ways in which they may be exercised and enjoyed.

METHODS. In educating the individual for freedom, a fifth branch of the educative process is required, namely, educational methods. Methods are the means whereby child nature may be guided in its development; the aims of education fulfilled; the functions of formal educational agencies discharged; and the content, activities, and experiences provided by the curriculum effected. Indeed, every aspect of the educative process depends on the choice and execution of correct methods to attain full fruition. Thus, also, the educational implementation of the Four Freedoms necessitates the right use of appropriate methods to guarantee full understanding and enjoyment of those freedoms.

Method has a narrow and a broad meaning. In the former, it is restricted to the use of devices and techniques. In the broad meaning it concerns the direction of the total responses of the child to attain specific goals. The following definition includes both the narrow and the broad meaning:

By method is meant the systematic way in which a teacher puts educative agents to work on human beings in order to produce certain desirable changes or results.

Desirable changes are those that make for human excellence in this life, and that contribute to man's final end and highest good. Evidences of such changes can be observed: (1) in the increase of worth-while knowledge by pupils; (2) in the pupil's development of right habits, interests, attitudes, and ideals; (3) in greater integration of the pupil's personality; (4) in the formation of the pupil's character through the knowledge and the practice of morality and religion; and (5) in the correct understanding and right use of freedom in pupils' daily lives.

It should be iterated that the major function of educational methods in the implementation of the Four Freedoms is to bring about those desirable changes or results which are most conducive to the proper exercise of those freedoms. When changes are consonant with man's dignity as a free being, are in harmony with the worth of human personality, and motivate perseverance in the pursuit of his sublime end, then, those changes are desirable and enhance the functioning of the Four Freedoms. On the other hand, changes which debase man's nature, imperil the attainment of his eternal destiny, frustrate the operation of his spiritual powers, and distort the true purposes of society, these are undesirable changes and tend to destroy the Four Freedoms.

Implementation of the Four Freedoms

The five aspects of the educative process discussed in the foregoing pages, when correctly interpreted, constitute right education. Each of the Four Freedoms can be implemented, more or less, under each aspect provided that these essential conditions are present: (1) The rank and file of teachers, as well as educational leaders generally, must believe in the intrinsic worth of those freedoms and the necessity for carrying them out in the daily business of the school. (2) The proximate aims or objectives of education must specifically express those freedoms. (3) The curriculum must include in its content and materials that necessary knowledge, and provide for those attitudes and appreciations, especially in the field of the social studies, which make those freedoms real and meaningful in the life of the pupil. (4) Each of the secondary agencies of education must contribute its share both in safeguarding those freedoms against all who would seek to deny or forbid them, and in using whatever legitimate means are at hand to make them possible of realization by the individual himself. (5) The teacher in his methodology must keep continually in mind that it is his supreme task and high privilege, by resourcefulness and example, to give pupils the positive knowledge of the worth of those freedoms and opportunity for their effective practice in everyday situations.

Freedom of speech and expression is furthered when the functional and consumer aspects of the educational offering are emphasized rather than the structural and producer aspects. This does not mean that only the useful and the pragmatic are to be desired in the training of youth. It does mean, however, that the pupil should be taught how to see relationships of cause and effect, how the content, materials and experiences of the curriculum function in actual life situations, and how, fortified with this functional or consumer knowledge, he can take his place in the social group and pursue his legitimate purposes and vocational needs. Thus, in the field of languages, art, music, the social studies, etc., the child must be given opportunity for self-realization so that he may form ideas and express them creatively, in conformity, of course, with approved standards governing the exercise of this freedom, common courtesy, and the moral law.

Freedom of religion is implemented when the pupil is neither subjected to nor indoctrinated in false and pernicious teachings, and when the school makes every reasonable provision for him to pursue his religious convictions and obligations, as is done in many localities today through the medium of "released time" for religious instruction. This freedom is promoted, also, when the curriculum is so constructed and organized as to include "religious materials," and when it is purged of content and experiences which are opposed to fundamental religious truths, such as the existence of God, the immortality of the soul, the freedom of the will, and man's redemption by Jesus Christ. Under this freedom, by appropriate aims and methods, the child is led to the truth, his intellect stimulated to accept it, and his will so enlightened and strengthened that consent in conduct is readily given to the true and the good.

Freedom from want is implemented when the pupil is equipped through instruction and discipline to seek the legitimate satisfaction of his physical, intellectual, vocational, and spiritual needs. This means that education must help the child to become self-supporting and self-directing, while he keeps in mind, at the same time, his obligation to contribute to the common good and the amelioration of society. Thus the school should teach him not only "the causes of poverty" but also how to evaluate human wants, and how to set up valid standards by which they may be judged. In this way the child establishes for himself a scale of values in human living, and may, perhaps, grasp the wisdom of Oliver Goldsmith: "Man wants but little here below, nor wants that little long."

There are those who think that freedom from fear means only freedom from war, freedom from "the unjust aggressor." This is merely a partial view of the meaning of that particular freedom. The injunction of Christ, "Fear not," must be applied to *every* condition and situation of life. Freedom from fear can be achieved by education only when the child is given that instruction and necessary training which positively acquaints him with what he is properly to fear and what not to fear. This resolves itself into a purposeful effort to have him apply in his daily living the teachings of true religion and the principles of sound mental hygiene. The child thereby is prepared to face reality, and to effect an intelligent solution of his individual and social problems in a manner that provides him with maximum security.

FREEDOM AND THE TEACHER. Traditionally considered, the term "academic freedom" has a twofold application: freedom for the teacher, and freedom for the student. These freedoms are commonly expressed, respectively, by the words *Lehrfreiheit* and *Lernfreiheit*. Of late years, emphasis has been placed mainly on *Lehrfreiheit,* freedom of the teacher, in the perennial battle for academic freedom. The term is usually interpreted to mean the right and the duty of a teacher to teach *truth*.

There is, of course, a body of objective truth made

known to man by divine revelation, which all men must accept for right living and for their eternal salvation. There is, in addition, a body of truth which makes up a part of "the social heritage." On both of these foundation stones of truth, Western Civilization is based. Seldom in defense of those truths, and more often in defiance of them, the cry of "academic freedom" is raised by certain groups of the professoriate. These groups proclaim as follows: "We start with no preconceptions; we accept no tradition; we recognize no authority, human or divine. We are independent thinkers and we claim the right to express ourselves untrammeled by any limitation except our own private judgment and individual interpretation."

In spite of the unwarranted claim of these professorial groups, it can be readily seen that truth, as such, does not lend itself to individual interpretation. In plain language it should be stated that no teacher has the right to disregard basic truth, or to interpret it according to his particular and peculiar fancy, or according to his own ignorance of its origin, worth, and authority. One must distinguish immediately, therefore, between academic freedom, properly so called, and academic license. Thus, academic freedom does not mean, as some mistaken and willful professors would have it mean, that any and every teacher or professor has the right to teach what he wants to teach in whatever way he wants to teach it, even assuming that his motives are profoundly sincere. To grant this wide latitude to any teacher would be granting him not freedom, but license rather. This is evident from the fact that, oftentimes, "what one wants to teach" may not be the truth. Indeed, it may be nothing more than individual

opinion, misinformation, inexact notions of fundamental principles and issues, an unfounded prejudice
or some personal conceit. Not infrequently, it may be
plain, unadulterated error.

Usually, those teachers who insist most vigorously
on the *right* of academic freedom are the same ones
who, basically ignorant of the true meaning of freedom
itself, abuse the very right which they so vehemently
demand. Their main concern, quite often, is to sell
their wares in the educational market place or to air
their personal views with solemn infallibility. Seldom
if ever do such teachers grant the right of academic
freedom to their students: the right of the student to
reject the teachers' errors.

Academic freedom, like freedom itself and all its
various forms, has certain limitations or controls placed
upon it by the very nature of things, as well as by social
necessity. These major controls may be grouped under
the following categories: (1) the obligation to teach
truth; (2) the American way of life; (3) the immaturity
of students; (4) institutional purpose or policy; (5) the
boundaries of one's field of specialization.

Each of these categories will now be considered
briefly:

1. THE OBLIGATION TO TEACH TRUTH. To teach
truth is a teacher's sacred duty. In creating man, God
gave him an intellect, the proper object of which is the
attainment of truth. In accepting error, then, and worse
still in teaching it, the professor does violence to his
own intellect, since he deprives it of its proper object.
Furthermore, since the proper object of the student's
intellect is, likewise, truth, the teacher does violence
to the student's intellect when he teaches him error.

If true education is the very foundation of the structure of society, as it is commonly agreed, and if both true philosophic and scientific knowledge is essential to the preservation and development of civilization, then it would be fatal for the teacher to make error instead of truth the aim and content of that education. Now, "independence of thought," so jealously guarded by the professoriate, is shown precisely by adherence to *truth* in teaching, and not by the acceptance and propagation of *error*. This does not mean that tentative hypotheses may not be put forth by teachers within the field of their competence, and that controversial issues which fall within their field may not be minutely examined and discussed. It does mean, however, that mere opinions should be labeled as mere opinions, not as facts; that hypotheses should be set forth as hypotheses, not as truths; and that *all* aspects of controversial issues which properly come within the purview of the teacher's field, should be made known and discussed as exhaustively and impartially as it is reasonably possible.

Thus, the teacher must live up to the sacred obligation to teach truth not only exteriorly, but interiorly as well. This interior regard for truth is manifested by his personal integrity and intellectual honesty. Finally, the obligation to teach truth imposes on the teacher the correlative obligation to avoid error, both in regard to himself and to his students. Hence, the teacher's academic freedom is limited in no uncertain way by the obligation to teach "the truth, the whole truth, and nothing but the truth."

2. THE AMERICAN WAY OF LIFE. From the earliest foundations of the Republic of the United States, the people have accepted and valiantly fought to defend

what is known as "the American way of life." This way
of life is founded on sound, philosophic, Christian
principles[10] which all intelligent men of good will accept
as fundamental in individual as well as in social, economic, and political life. These sound principles ought
to be accepted and revered by those who earn their living, and whose rights are protected, under the flag of the
United States and the American way of life. These principles set limits to the teacher's academic freedom. Since
education is the means of making known, perpetuating,
and implementing these principles, and since education,
in its right meaning, is the vital concern of teachers, it
follows that a limit is set, naturally, to the teacher's
right to free speech and expression wherever and whenever these principles are concerned. The teacher, therefore, has no more right to teach the overthrow of the
American form of government and life, and to advocate
in its stead a collectivistic communistic form, than he
has a right to teach the excellence of anarchy, or the
benefits to be derived from mass suicide, or racial and
religious extinction.

Since these American principles are truths in themselves, because they conform to all the touchstones of
truth, and are supported in their major aspects by
Christian philosophy, they set a limit to academic freedom in the United States, which limit the teacher has
the obligation to recognize and observe. This is not
at all to say that the teacher has not the right and the
duty to examine these principles, and the added duty
of seeing in what specific ways he can the more immediately implement them in his own life and environ-

<hr>

[10] Cf. Walsh, J. J., *Education of the Founding Fathers of the Republic* (New York: Fordham University Press, 1935), Preface, p. x.

ment. But when he attempts to tear down those principles, to belittle them, to regard them as "old fashioned," unprogressive, and as clogs in the wheels of progress, he is not exercising his right to academic freedom; on the contrary, he is guilty of academic license.

3. THE MATURITY OF STUDENTS. On page 182 it was pointed out that the proper object of the intellect is *truth*. The student, then, because of his immaturity, needs the influence of the mature, informed mind of the adult over his own immature mind in assisting it to attain truth. Such influence should always be honest and wholesome. This means that *truth* not *error* should be offered to the student's intellect, and that *good* should be presented to his will so that he may learn how to make proper choices. The teacher, therefore, is limited in his freedom of teaching by the very immaturity of the student himself: He must present truth to the student's intellect, good to his will, and the highest forms of beauty for his enjoyment and appreciation. Furthermore, the teacher must adapt his teaching to the level of the student's physical, social, and mental development. He must not take advantage of the student's immaturity, and, therefore, must refrain from presenting points of view that are colored by his own prejudices, or that the student cannot grasp in their entirety until development has progressed to a more complete stage. Nor is this all; for the teacher, at certain levels of student growth, must insist that the student accept truth, for the moment, on the *sole* authority of the teacher himself. As stated in Chapter I, this is the substitutional function of authority, and contributes to the exercise of freedom rightly interpreted.

Thus, the teacher's academic freedom is limited by the immaturity of the student; by the fact that specific obligations to the student rest upon the teacher because of that immaturity; and by the added fact that the teacher must respect the intellect of the student, the proper object of which is *truth*.

4. INSTITUTIONAL CONTROL. Educational institutions, whether state or denominational, exist for specific purposes, and have a definite, legitimate policy which it is their function to carry out. Both the purpose and the policy of such institutions limit the freedom of the teacher in the content and scope of his teaching. Catholic institutions, in particular, have a body of truth that comes both from divine revelation and from tradition, which it is the duty of teacher and student alike to accept and respect.

5. THE BOUNDARIES OF ONE'S FIELD. While wide latitude is usually extended to the teacher in his own especial field, wherein by his preparation and training he is supposed to be somewhat expert, nevertheless, he may not speak with authority outside the limits of his own field. In his discussions of controversial subjects or issues that lie outside his province, and in which he has no professional competence, the teacher is quite definitely restricted. Of course, there are professors, here and there, who vainly imagine themselves experts in every field. In their own fancy, they assume to themselves the dictum of the old Roman: "Nothing human is foreign to me." Such professors, fortunately, are not too often encountered, and one can usually observe that they are "touched by a certain madness."

EDUCATION AND THE SOCIAL ORDER. It is evident at once that, for the implementation of the Four Freedoms, there is needed also a social order constructed on the principles of the Christian, democratic way of life. Through ignorance, neglect, or willful exclusion, however, certain individuals, groups, and nations, do not accept and conform their conduct to this way of life. For that very reason, the work of true education has a distinct role to fulfill in promoting the Four Freedoms when the turmoil of the present world conflict has passed, and peace has been restored to the nations of the world.

The question may well be asked, therefore, "What kind of world is needed in order that these freedoms may function effectively?" The answer to this question is: *a world that is constructed in conformity to God's law and that fosters man's complete development, material and spiritual, in accordance with that law.* That kind of world ought to include, among other things, the recognition of individual freedom as a gift of God; respect for the inalienable rights of the individual; knowledge of man's brotherhood and spiritual equality; and the acceptance of absolute, universal, moral principles governing all aspects of life. Education, then, should seek to inculcate in the individual the foregoing fundamental truths if it is to effect desirable changes in the individual and, consequently, in the social order.

Certain social conditions are also necessary for the actualization of the Four Freedoms. The most important of these may be stated categorically as follows:

1. SECURITY. This implies that measure of physical, political, economic, moral, and religious independence and protection which will permit men to pursue their legitimate interests and ends without interference or danger of violence from any public or private source.

This condition requires proper limitations on freedom and definite restraints on the exercise of unreasonable authority.

2. PRODUCTIVITY. This condition requires that moral principles be applied to society in such manner that an economic-scientific plan for distribution of the materials and resources of the world be effected which will ward off famine and pestilence, and remove the possibility of involuntary poverty by peoples and nations less favored by nature in material goods. Education, in seeking safeguards against stark want, must favor the control of economic forces and laws by subjecting them to the guidance of authoritative moral principles.

3. ECONOMY. This condition expresses the patent need for the correct use of individual talents and vocational capabilities to promote the temporal welfare of all through assuaging economic ills and social injustices. Economy thus contributes to the moral amelioration of society by the full and fruitful use of all human resources and materials. Such economy constitutes a demand which education ought to strive to attain in the world of business, industry, commerce, and international relations, if freedom is to receive adequate expression. Education should seek, moreover, to equip each individual to participate fully in the promotion of the common good as intelligently and effectively as his abilities permit. This implies that everyone shall have opportunity to receive that necessary training which will enable him to plan his life and direct his activities, consonant, of course, with the moral law and the dictates of his own conscience, so that the general welfare is promoted, and his own betterment

enhanced. Economy does not imply that everyone should receive equal material reward for service to society, for such reward must be governed always by the quality and character of the services rendered. It does imply, however, that all honest human endeavor must receive a just return.

4. EQUITY. This means that state of moral, social, economic justice which gives expression to the lawful demands of human nature, man's inalienable rights and duties, freedom and authority, to all of which an objective scale of values must be applied if man and society are to fulfill their ordained purposes. The moral law supplies this scale of values and is applicable in all situations governing the individual and society.

5. BEAUTY. By this is meant the combination of truth and goodness merged in individual and social conduct, in the environment, and in the refined elements of civilization and culture, which gives the individual a certain sense of contemplated satisfaction and pleasure. Because of this pleasure derived from the merging of the true and the good in conduct, the individual strives earnestly with perseverance toward the advancement of himself aesthetically, as well as of society, in conformity to the eternal norms of morality.

6. TOLERANCE. This condition implies the intellectual state of understanding and appreciating the individual's common origin, nature, end, and inalienable rights, regardless of his individual differences. These differences must be permitted expression without interference, provided such expression does no violence to the individual himself, and does not conflict with the moral law governing conduct and the exercise of

the Four Freedoms. But in no sense whatsoever may tolerance be correctly interpreted to mean indifference to error, to right and wrong, and passivity toward their existence.

Even when all six of these social conditions necessary for the Four Freedoms are more or less present in the social order, it must be emphasized further that no one should be condemned to a life of mechanical routine, or confined to a narrow range of intellectual development, through lack of education. On the contrary, through the medium of right education, man's freedom receives correct implementation, and thereby serves to equip him for his legitimate life activities, whatever they may be. Some individuals are endowed with talents which make for leadership; others are more fitted for followership. In either case, education should serve to enable the individual to contribute to the advancement of society, in some measure at least, and facilitate the attainment of his own material and spiritual purposes.

It should be remembered always that, in truth and fact, the Four Freedoms represent an ideal, a blueprint, as it were, of a better world. Education, if rightly interpreted and applied, is a means of attaining that better world by its power to make known what those freedoms really mean and how the individual may properly put them into practice. Those freedoms, however, are limited in their effectiveness by the individual's *will to achieve* them, and, equally, by his will to exercise them properly. Hence, they are fruitful only in so far as the character of the individual himself is fruitful and steadfast. The individual is free. Education can acquaint him with the meaning of his freedom and how he can exercise it best for his own and for the common good.

But only the individual himself can *will* to apply his knowledge of its meaning and make it function in his daily living. No one can really free him except himself alone. "Qui potest capere, capiat." (He who can attain it, let him attain it.)

SELECTED BIBLIOGRAPHY

Agar, W. M., *Catholicism and the Philosophy of Natural Science* (New York: The Macmillan Co., 1941).

American Council on Public Affairs, *Education and the United Nations* (Washington, D. C.: American Council on Public Affairs, 1943).

Beale, H. K., *Are American Teachers Free?* (New York: Charles Scribner's Sons, 1936).

Bellerby, J. R., *Economic Reconstruction* (New York: The Macmillan Co., 1943).

Best, H., *The Soviet Experiment* (New York: R. R. Smith, 1941).

Beveridge, W. H., *The Pillars of Security* (New York: The Macmillan Co., 1943).

—— *Social Insurance and Allied Services* (New York: The Macmillan Co., 1943).

Bobbitt, F., *The Curriculum of Modern Education* (New York: McGraw-Hill Book Co., Inc., 1941).

Bode, B., *Democracy As a Way of Life* (New York: The Macmillan Co., 1937).

Brauer, T. (Ed.) et al. *Thomistic Principles in a Catholic School* (St. Louis: B. Herder Book Co., 1943).

Breed, F. S., *Education and the New Realism* (New York: The Macmillan Co., 1939).

Brubacher, J. S., *Modern Philosophies of Education* (New York: McGraw-Hill Book Co., Inc., 1939).

Campbell, F. S., *The Menace of the Herd* (Milwaukee: The Bruce Publishing Co., 1943).

Carmichael, P. A., "The Test of Academic Freedom," *Bulletin, American Association of University Professors,* Vol. 29, No. 3, June, 1943, pp. 373–384.

Case, S. J., *The Christian Philosophy of History* (Chicago: University of Chicago Press, 1943).

Childs, J. L., *Education and the Philosophy of Experimentalism* (New York: The Century Co., 1931).

—— "Experimentalism and American Education," *Teachers College Record*, Vol. XLIV, May, 1943, pp. 539–543.

Cronin, J. T., *A Basic Plan for Catholic Curriculum Construction*, Doctoral Dissertation (Washington, D. C.: The Catholic University of America, 1927).

—— *The Function of Principles and Methods in Education*, Radio Address, Station WNYC New York, April 1, 1936.

—— *The Individual Versus Society* (New York: Private Printing, Fordham University Graduate School, Division of Administration and Methods, 1937).

Deferrari, R. J. (Ed.), *Essays on Catholic Education in the United States* (Washington, D. C.: The Catholic University of America Press, 1942).

de Schweinitz, K., *England's Road to Social Security* (Philadelphia, Pa.: University of Pennsylvania Press, 1943).

Dewey, J., *Freedom and Culture* (New York: G. P. Putnam's Sons, 1939).

—— *Democracy and Education* (New York: The Macmillan Co., 1916).

—— *Experience and Education* (New York: The Macmillan Co., 1938).

Donat, J., *Freedom of Science* (New York: J. F. Wagner, 1914).

Eastman, M., "We Must Face the Facts About Russia," *The Readers Digest*, Vol. 43, No. 255, July, 1943.

Educational Freedom and Democracy: The Second Yearbook of the John Dewey Society (New York: Teachers College, Columbia University, 1939).

Educational Policies Commission, *Education and the People's Peace* (Washington, D. C.: National Education Association of the United States and the American Association of School Administrators, 1943).

—— *The Education of Free Men in American Democracy* (Washington, D. C.: National Education Association, 1941).

Eliot, T. S., *The Idea of a Christian Society* (London: Faber and Faber, Ltd., 1939).

Farrell, W., *A Companion to the Summa* (New York: Sheed and Ward, Vol. I, 1941; Vol. II, 1939).

Flewelling, R. T., *The Survival of Western Culture* (New York: Harper & Brothers, 1943).

Forty-First Yearbook, National Society for the Study of Education. "Philosophies of Education," Part I (Bloomington, Ill.: Public School Publishing Co., 1942).

Furfey, P. H., *A History of Social Thought* (New York: The Macmillan Co., 1942).

Gannon, R. I., *God in Education* (New York: The Paulist Press, 1943).

Gauss, C., "Can We Educate for Democracy?" *Bulletin of the American Association of University Professors,* Vol. 28, No. 5, Dec., 1942, pp. 610–624.

Giordani, I., *The Social Message of Jesus* (Paterson, N. J.: St. Anthony Guild Press, 1943).

Greenwalt, W. E., *Democracy's Salvation* (Denver, Colo.: The World Press, 1943).

Guinan, Sr. M. Angelica, *Freedom and Authority in Education,* Doctoral Dissertation (Washington, D. C.: The Catholic University of America, 1936).

Guthrie, H., "Education for the Christian Individual," *A Philosophical Symposium on American Catholic Education* (New York: Fordham University Press, 1941).

Gwynn, J. M., *Curriculum Principles and Social Trends* (New York: The Macmillan Co., 1943).

Hart, C. A. (Ed.), *Philosophy and Order* (Washington, D. C.: The American Catholic Philosophical Association, The Catholic University of America, 1942).

——— *Proceedings of the American Catholic Philosophical Association,* "The Problem of Liberty" (Washington, D. C.: The Catholic University of America, 1940), Vol. XVI.

Hemleben, S. J., *Plans for World Peace Through Six Centuries* (Chicago: University of Chicago Press, 1943).

Hoffman, R., *Tradition and Progress* (Milwaukee: The Bruce Publishing Co., 1938).

Holmes, H. W., *The Road to Courage* (New York: Alfred A. Knopf, 1942).

Hopkins, L. T., *Interaction: The Democratic Process* (Boston: D. C. Heath and Co., 1941).

Horne, H. H., *The Democratic Philosophy of Education* (New York: The Macmillan Co., 1932).

——— *The Philosophy of Christian Education* (New York: F. H. Revell Co., 1937).

Hoyt, E. E., *Freedom From Want: A World Goal* (New York: Public Affairs Committee, 30 Rockefeller Plaza, 1943).

Husslein, J., *Social Wellsprings* (Milwaukee: The Bruce Publishing Co., 1940, Vol. I, 1942, Vol. II).

Hutchins, R. M., *Education for Freedom* (Baton Rouge, La.: Louisiana State University Press, 1943).

——— "Toward a Durable Society," *American Association of University Professors Bulletin,* Vol. XXIX, No. 4, Oct., 1943, pp. 467–482.

Jacobs, I. T., and De Boer, J. J., *Educating for Peace* (New York: D. Appleton-Century Co., 1940).

Jordan, H. P. (Ed.), *Problems of Post-War Reconstruction* (Washington, D. C.: American Council on Public Affairs, 1943).

Kandel, I., *The End of an Era* (New York: Bureau of Publications, Columbia University, 1941).

Kane, W., *Some Principles of Education* (Chicago: Loyola University Press, 1938).

Kerby, W. J., *The Social Mission of Charity* (New York: The Macmillan Co., 1930).

Kerwin, J. G., "Public Concerns of an American Catholic," *Social Problems,* Vol. I, No. 7, September, 1938.

Knellar, G. F., *The Educational Philosophy of National Socialism* (New Haven: Yale University Press, 1941).

Knight, E. W., *Progress and Educational Perspective* (New York: The Macmillan Co., 1942).

Koenig, H. C. (Ed.), *Principles for Peace* (Milwaukee: The Bruce Publishing Co., 1943).

Kohn, H., *World Order in Historical Perspective* (Cambridge: Harvard University Press, 1942).

Leo XIII, *The Great Encyclical Letters of Leo XIII* (New York: Benziger Bros., 1903).

Leonard, J. P., and Eurich, A. C., *An Evaluation of Modern Education* (New York: D. Appleton-Century Co., 1942).

Lindsay, A. D., *Religion, Science and Society in the Modern World* (New Haven: Yale University Press, 1943).

Livingstone, R., *Education for a World Adrift* (New York: The Macmillan Co., 1943).

Lodge, R. C., *Philosophy of Education* (New York: Harper & Bros., 1937).

Mac Iver, R. M., *Towards An Abiding Peace* (New York: The Macmillan Co., 1943).

Marinoff, I., *The Heresy of National Socialism* (London: Burns, Oates and Washburne, Ltd., 1941).

Maritain, J., *Education at the Crossroads* (New York: Yale University Press, 1943).

—— *Freedom in the Modern World* (New York: Charles Scribner's Sons, 1938).

—— *The Rights of Man and the Natural Law* (New York: Charles Scribner's Sons, 1943).

—— *Scholasticism and Politics* (New York: The Macmillan Co., 1941).

—— *Twilight of Civilization* (Trans. by L. Landry) (New York: Sheed and Ward, 1943).

Massimi, M. (Cardinal) *Catholic Morality* (Trans. by J. I. Schade) (Patterson, N. J.: St. Anthony Guild Press, 1943).

McCarthy, R. C., *Training the Adolescent* (Milwaukee: The Bruce Publishing Co., 1934).

McConnell, J. W., *The Basic Teachings of the Great Economists* (New York: The New Home Library, 1943).

McFadden, C. J., *The Philosophy of Communism* (New York: Benziger Bros., 1939).

McGovern, W. M., *From Luther to Hitler* (Boston: Houghton-Mifflin Co., 1941).

McMahon, J. T., *Building Character From Within* (Milwaukee: The Bruce Publishing Co., 1940).

McNabb, V., *Old Principles and the New Order* (New York: Sheed and Ward, 1942).

McWilliams, J. S., *Philosophy for the Millions* (New York: The Macmillan Co., 1942).

Millar, M. F. X., "The American Concept of Man," *Thought*, Vol. XVII, No. 67, Dec., 1942, pp. 667–684.

Mursell, J. L., *Education for American Democracy* (New York: W. W. Norton & Co., 1943).

Nef, J. U., *The United States and Civilization* (Chicago: University of Chicago Press, 1942).

Nichols, R. F., and Nichols, J. P., *A Short History of American Democracy* (New York: D. Appleton-Century Company, 1943).

Noyes, C. E., *Economic Freedom* (New York: Harper & Brothers, 1943).

O'Brien, Sr. M. C., *Christian Social Principles* (New York: P. J. Kenedy and Sons, 1941).

O'Connell, G., *Naturalism in American Education* (New York: Benziger Bros., 1938).

Osgniach, A. J., *The Christian State* (Milwaukee: The Bruce Publishing Co., 1943).

O'Shaughnessy, M., *Peace and Reconstruction* (New York: Harper & Bros., 1943).

Parkes, H. B., *The Pragmatic Test, Essays on the History of Ideas* (San Francisco: The Colt Press, 1941).

Perry, C. M., *The Philosophy of Democracy* (Chicago: University of Chicago Press, 1943).

Peters, C. C., *The Curriculum of Democratic Education* (New York: McGraw-Hill Book Co., Inc., 1942).

Philosophy of the State: Proceedings of the American Catholic Philosophical Association, Volume XV (Washington, D. C.: The Catholic University of America, 1939).

Pittinger, B. F., *Indoctrination for American Democracy* (New York: The Macmillan Co., 1941).

Pius XI, *On Atheistic Communism* (New York: The America Press, 1937).

―― *The Christian Education of Youth* (New York: The America Press, 1936).

―― *On the Reconstruction of the Social Order* (New York: The America Press, 1938).

Pius XII, *The Unity of Human Society* (New York: The America Press, 1939).

Pratt, J. B., *Naturalism* (New Haven: Yale University Press, 1938).

"Progressive Education . . . Its Philosophy and Challenge," *Progressive Education*, Vol. 18, No. 5, May, 1941.

Redden, J. D., and Ryan, F. A., *A Catholic Philosophy of Education* (Milwaukee: The Bruce Publishing Co., 1942).

Report to the Commission on Liberal Education of the Association of American Colleges, "The Post-War Responsibilities of Liberal Education," *Bulletin, American Association of University Professors*, Vol. 29, No. 3, June, 1943, pp. 412–431.

Reynolds, G. F., and Connors, D. F., *Freedom Speaks* (New York: The Ronald Press Company, 1943).

Roche, P. J., *Democracy in the Light of Four Current Educational Philosophies*, Doctoral Dissertation (Washington, D. C.: The Catholic University of America, 1942).

Ruland, L., *Morality and the Social Order* (St. Louis: B. Herder Book Co., 1942).

Russell, C. E. B., *The Path of Reconstruction* (New York: Henry Holt & Co., 1942).

Ryan, J. A., and Millar, M., *The State and Church* (New York: The Macmillan Co., 1937).

Scherman, H., *The Last Best Hope of Earth* (New York: Random House, 1941).

Schumpeter, J. A., *Capitalism, Socialism and Democracy* (New York: Harper & Brothers, 1942).

Schwer, W., *Catholic Social Theory* (St. Louis: B. Herder Book Co., 1940).

Science, Philosophy, and Religion, Third Symposium (New York: The Conference on Science, Philosophy, and Religion in Their Relation to the Democratic Way of Life, Inc., 1943).

Sheldon, W. H., *America's Progressive Philosophy* (New Haven: Yale University Press, 1942).

Simon, E. P., *Strong As the People* (New York: Friendship House, 1943).

Simon, Y., *Nature and Function of Authority* (Milwaukee: Marquette University Press, 1940).

Sheed, F., *Communism and Man* (London: Sheed and Ward, 1938).

Sheen, F. J., *A Declaration of Dependence* (Milwaukee: The Bruce Publishing Co., 1941).

—— *Freedom Under God* (Milwaukee: The Bruce Publishing Co., 1940).

Smith, M. J., *John Dewey and Moral Education* (Washington, D. C.: Guthrie Lithograph Co., 1939).

Smith, T. V., *Discipline for Democracy* (Chapel Hill: University of North Carolina Press, 1942).

Spellman, F. J., *The Road to Victory* (New York: Charles Scribner's Sons, 1942).

—— *Action This Day* (New York: Charles Scribner's Sons, 1943).

St. Thomas Aquinas, *Summa Theologica* (London: Burns, Oates and Washbourne, Ltd., 1927), Vol. IV.

—— *De Regimine Principum* (Taurini, Italy: Petri Marietti, 1924).

Sturmthal, A., *A Survey of Literature on Post-War Reconstruction* (New York: New York University, Institute of Post-War Reconstruction, 1943).

Sturzo, L., *Politics and Morality* (London: Burns, Oates and Washbourne, Ltd., 1938).

—— *The True Life* (Washington, D. C.: The Catholic University of America, 1943).

Teachers for Democracy: Fourth Yearbook of the John

Dewey Society (New York: D. Appleton-Century Co., 1940).

Wallace, H. A., *America's Part in World Reconstruction* (New York: The Woodrow Wilson Foundation, 1943).

—— *The Century of the Common Man* (New York: Reynal & Hitchcock, 1943).

Walsh, G., *Medieval Humanism* (New York: The Macmillan Co., 1942).

—— "Humanism and Peace," *Thought,* Vol. XVIII, No. 68, March, 1943, pp. 101–109.

Walsh, J. J., *Education of the Founding Fathers of the Republic* (New York: Fordham University Press, 1935).

Welles, S., *The World of the Four Freedoms* (New York: Columbia University Press, 1943).

Wheat, C. E. (Ed.) *The Democratic Tradition in America* (Boston: Ginn & Co., 1943).

Wood, H. G., *Christianity and Civilization* (New York: The Macmillan Co., 1943).

Woodlock, T. F., *The Catholic Pattern* (New York: Simon and Schuster, Inc., 1942).

Woody, C. (Ed.) *The Discipline of Practical Judgment in a Democratic Society* (Chicago: The University of Chicago Press, 1943).

Wriston, H. M., *Challenge to Freedom* (New York: Harper & Brothers, 1943).

Yat-Sen, S., *San Miu Chu I* (The Three Principles of the People), Trans. by Price, F. W., Edited by Chen, L. T. (Chungking, China: Ministry of Information of the Republic of China, 1943).

Yutang, L., *Between Tears and Laughter* (New York: The John Day Company, 1943).

INDEX

A